NO REGRETS

NO REGRETS

The Earl of Carnarvon

Weidenfeld and Nicolson
London

To my dear friend, Crystal

First impression November 1976
Second impression November 1976
Third impression January 1977
Fourth impression February 1977
Fifth impression March 1978

Published by George Weidenfeld and Nicolson Limited,
11 St John's Hill, London SW11.

ISBN 0 297 77246 5

Printed in Great Britain by
Butler & Tanner Ltd, Frome and London

Contents

Illustrations

Acknowledgments

The author and publisher are grateful to the following sources for their kind permission to reproduce the illustrations: for illustration number 3, Aerofilms Ltd; 5, Sport and General, and 6, Sir Cecil Beaton.

The author would like to express his gratitude to Major-General Roger Evans whose excellent book *The Years Between* helped him in relating the incidents of the Mesopotamian and Turkish campaigns.

I
Happy Highclere

Kind reader, for what you are about to receive, I make no apologies. I trust that you will be interested and amused by the tales of an era in which life was mostly fun and frolic. Notwithstanding the many follies that I have committed, I must confess that, on balance, I have no regrets.

I was born at the end of the naughty nineties when Queen Victoria was on the throne and the Prince of Wales was the leader of the gay society of that era. My father was the fifth Earl of Carnarvon and so as his son and heir I received the courtesy title of Lord Porchester; as a result I was known to all my friends as Porchey. My father usually called me Porchester unless exceptionally and quite unusually pleased when he would suddenly seem to remember that he had originally bestowed the name of Henry upon me. Sadly my father and I were never very close but we did share a great mutual love for our home Highclere.

Highclere has been in the Herbert family since the eighteenth century and all the best memories of my childhood are centred upon it. One of the great houses of England, its close-cropped lawns were shaded by giant cedars: these in their turn were surrounded by thickets of hawthorn, woods of beech and oak and lakes full of wildfowl. All around stood the high downs, some densely timbered, others bare chalk.

In the reign of Edward VI the Crown took possession of the manor of Highclere and granted it to the Fitzwilliam family. It then passed through the Kingsmills and the Lucys of Warwickshire until it was purchased in 1659 by Sir Robert Sawyer, Attorney General to Charles II and James II.

Highclere Placehouse was at this time a double-fronted Elizabethan brick mansion, with a courtyard, barns, stables, a dovecote, large garden, two kitchen gardens and two orchards. Sir Robert lived at Highclere for thirteen years and in 1684 his daughter and heiress married the eighth Earl of Pembroke. Upon his mother's death in 1706 their second son, the Honourable Robert Herbert, succeeded to Highclere and it was he who built the follies still standing in the grounds known as Jackdaw's Castle, Heaven's Gate and the Temple, also part of Milford Lake House.

He was succeeded in turn by his nephew Henry Herbert, who became Lord of the Manor of Highclere in 1769. He constructed the large lake known as Dunsmere and by clever planting of trees and shrubs made the park a place of great beauty renowned throughout England. His cousin the Earl of Pembroke and Montgomery, living at Wilton, heard of his efforts and wrote to him in 1770:

> My dear Henry,
>
> I propose sending you four hundred exotic tree seedlings called Cedars of Lebanon which we have raised from cones brought to England by Bishop Pococke. I will send them by bullock cart so that they should reach you in two or three days. I trust you will enjoy planting them in your garden and other parts of your estate.

He received a reply which he felt was somewhat ungrateful.

> Dear Cousin,
>
> I thank you most kindly for your nice offer but I pray you, while you are about it, send four thousand as I have plenty of room in my Park.

This letter occasioned a sharp rebuke stating that he was lucky to be receiving any at all.

In 1793 Henry Herbert was created Earl of Carnarvon. Although he was known as the First Earl and indeed was the first one to live at Highclere, there had in fact been a previous Earl of Carnarvon but he had not lived long. This original Earl had been a distant relation, a son-in-law of the fourth Earl of Pembroke; he had also been a leading royalist and cavalry officer in the army of Charles I. After the Battle of Newbury in 1643, King Charles was resting in his headquarters at the Bear Inn, Hungerford, when an officer entered and said: 'Sire, we bring grave news. Outside lie the bodies of the Earls of Carnarvon, Falkland and Sunderland.' Whereupon the King threw his hands up in dismay: 'I can't bear it. I can't bear it. All is lost. We must flee.' And so saying, he mounted his horse and galloped away towards Bath.

Henry Herbert, the first Earl to live at Highclere, was succeeded by his son in 1811. The Second Earl continued the development of the Park and was largely responsible for the vast plantings of azaleas and rhododendrons whose colours in their season are a glorious sight. Upon his death in 1833 his son Henry John George became the Third Earl and it was he who conceived Highclere Castle as it stands today.

This Third Earl was a great traveller and spent much of his early life abroad, but in later years he settled at Highclere and devoted himself almost entirely to reconstruction. He engaged the services of Sir Charles Barry, architect of the Houses of Parliament, to help him and between them they turned Highclere House into Highclere Castle.

After much preparation, alteration and submission of designs, the final plan was decided upon, and work began in 1839. At this time, a master stonemason received fourteen shillings a week and an ordinary stonemason seven shillings a week. But one should remember that a large cottage loaf cost one penny and a pint of beer a halfpenny.

During the three years the work took to complete, Highclere was a place of great activity as oxen drew hundreds of cartloads of stone the many miles from the quarries at Bath. Sir Charles Barry had advised against the use of Bath stone, saying he could only guarantee it for one hundred years; but his patron was adamant, saying that that would be sufficient for his lifetime.

The stone used has certainly suffered from the weather and many of the pinnacles have broken off. Nevertheless, at the time of writing, the walls, some of which are sixteen feet thick, guarantee that Highclere is in no danger of disappearing for the next few centuries, so much the better as it had cost my ancestor £240,000 to complete.

Roly Cubitt, of Holland, Hannen & Cubitt, spent a weekend here about twenty years ago. He said he would very much enjoy making a rough estimate of what it would cost his firm to put up a building such as this. Fortunately, he had his instruments with him and he told me that although, of course, stonemasons no longer existed, it would cost approximately three million pounds to do the job.

With the main house uninhabitable while the work was being carried out, Henry John and his family retired to the small eighteenth-century house at Milford which Robert Herbert had built. Henry John loved hunting, and returning home after a good day's sport he asked his servant to pull off his boots and put a chair outside so that he could enjoy the sunset with a glass of port. 'Bring me a rug and call me in half an hour.' When the man returned, it was to find that the Third Earl had apparently fallen asleep. He nudged him gently: 'M'Lord, are you awake?' He tried yet again, then realized that his master was dead. It was a good way to go: none better. He was succeeded in turn by my grandfather who was a great statesman and scholar, holding office as Secretary of State for the Colonies and Lord Lieutenant of Ireland.

His son, my father, was born in 1866 and succeeded in 1889 when he was only twenty-three. His sister considered him 'a great tease, a terrific tease, then and to the end of his life, in sober middle age getting the same rapture from a prank carried out on his friends or family as a fifth form schoolboy. He was blessed with a courage that was of that peculiar calm variety which means a pleasurable quickening of the pulse in the hour of danger.'

On one occasion in his youth he hired a boat to take him somewhere off the coast of Italy to his yacht lying out at sea. He was alone, steering the little boat rowed by a couple of fishermen. Suddenly, when far removed from land and equally distant from his goal, the two men gave him a choice between payment of a large sum or being pitched into the water. He listened quietly and motioned to them to pass his dressing bag. They obeyed, already in imagination fingering the English Lord's ransom. However, the situation was reversed when, instead of extracting a well-stuffed pocket book, he pulled out a revolver and pointing it at the two men bade them row on or he would shoot.

One of the best shots in England, he also enjoyed golf, horse racing, music, travel and Egyptology. Except when his passion for sport kept him at home during the shooting season and his love of opera for a few weeks in London in the summer, he would be off on his travels, suddenly dashing off to Paris or Constantinople, Egypt or Sweden, Italy or Berlin for long or short periods, returning home equally unexpectedly, having collected pictures and books and any number of acquaintances and friends.

In about 1890, my father took up his interest in horse racing and soon became deeply involved, for he was incapable of doing anything half-heartedly. Ultimately, his main effort was directed toward his Stud Farm which he started in 1902 and with horses bred there, he won many of the big races of the period, among them the Ascot Stakes, the Stewards' Cup at Goodwood, the Doncaster Cup, the City and Suburban and others.

Apart from his friendships with those of his own world, he was genuinely interested in the many personalities known to him one and all by nicknames he never forgot.

When the spare figure appeared in the paddock on a

racecourse, wearing a unique sort of low-crowned felt hat, of a shape never seen on any head but his own, and a frayed bow tie, shod, whatever the smartness of the occasion, with brown shoes – 'that fellow's damn brown shoes', as a great personage once observed – he could count on a special welcome.

A pioneer of motoring, my father was one of the first to own a car. Many pedestrians were said to have shaken their fists at him and shouted insulting remarks the first time they saw him travel slowly up Muswell Hill at about four miles an hour in his Panhard, preceded by a man with a red flag. No doubt they recognized what a noisy pest the infernal machine was to become.

He was a very good-looking man and all the Society hostesses of the day were extremely keen that he should marry one of their daughters. As it happened, he picked on my mother who was a very beautiful girl, the illegitimate daughter of Alfred de Rothschild and Mrs Wombwell. Alfred was a strict practising Jew and my grandmother, Marie Wombwell, was an ardent Roman Catholic: they could never get married because neither was prepared to change their religion, but they were a devoted couple and adored their only child Almina, who was petite, truly a pocket Venus who stood out from all her contemporaries.

My father, who always had an eye to the main chance, drove a hard bargain with Alfred and told him that he thought my mother should have a dowry, suggesting half-a-million pounds divided between them as a marriage settlement, so that if one predeceased the other, the surviving partner could do whatsoever he, or she, liked with the balance of the money. My father had, at that time, a lot of debts (approximately £150,000) and he also asked Alfred to pay off all these debts so that when they started married life, they could do so with a clean sheet. Alfred readily agreed.

They were married in 1895 and I was the first-born. Three years later my sister Eve arrived and became the apple of my father's eye – quite rightly so. He worshipped her and they were the closest of friends until he died. She had a great influence for good on him and healed many a breach between my father and mother which no-one but she could have achieved.

When he was married, whether living at Highclere or in London, my father always kept a good table. He employed a French chef and at one time he also had an Austrian pastry-cook who used to make the most delicious chocolate cakes in the world. They had Marquis chocolate outside with apricot jam in the middle. For a short period he even employed a Sinhalese cook solely to make curries of which he was inordinately fond. The head still-room maid produced excellent scones, rolls and ginger-snaps which were stuffed full of cream. She also had to make, in season, a wide range of jams and conserves of all kinds.

My father always had breakfast upstairs in his room. Normally, this consisted of two slices of toast which he spread thickly with clotted cream and a spoonful of guava jelly, hot coffee and, in season, a peach or a pear or even a good Cox's apple. He was reasonably abstemious and at lunch usually drank plain water or possibly a glass of white wine. At dinner, he had the habit of pouring a glass of sherry into his soup. After dinner, he always drank a lot of old brandy and invariably smoked half of an Egyptian cigarette, manufactured by Isherwood, through a Meerschaum and amber holder.

He never opened a letter as he detested that particular chore and George Fearnside, who was his valet for many years, would often find unopened letters that had lain on his desk for three or four months, particularly so if they appeared to be bills.

He had an aversion to cutting down trees, however ancient or dangerous they had become and planted very few. He also disliked interviews with his land agent, Rutherford, and when that poor man finally managed to obtain an interview, he was always greeted by the self-same words, 'Come on, Rutherford, what do you want? Get it over quickly!'

2
Infantile Escapades

My earliest recollections of Highclere were of a warm house that required the filling, trimming and lighting of one hundred and fifty-six oil lamps; and I can just recall my first introduction to a pony, upon which I rode strapped in a wicker pannier. My sister Evelyn and I lived on the top floor with Nanny Moss, our governess and nursemaids in a self-contained community, remote from our elders, to be seldom seen and never heard.

On those rare occasions when my parents would venture up to see us, usually at tea-time, we would spring to our feet and stand to attention in a silence that was awful and I never knew what to say. Suddenly my father would begin a monosyllabic conversation.

'Ho hm; by Jove, terribly hot in here ... very fuggy ... very fuggy indeed.' A pause as he would look around.

'Oh dear, goodness me,' as his eye lit upon our birdcage. 'No, no this will never do. It'll scatter birdseed all over the place and that will encourage the rats and mice. No, I think no more birds,' he would say emphatically, turning to our governess.

'Very well, m'Lord,' would come the timorous reply. Then, bravely, knowing our affection for the little canary,

'Of course, you are quite right, m'Lord, but do you think perhaps the cage could be kept in the bathroom? The children are very fond of their little bird and I know they would be most upset if it had to be taken away entirely.'

My father pondered the question as if reflecting on a great matter of State.

'Well, I suppose in the circumstances . . .' he would say, and the cage was moved to the bathroom.

Suddenly he would turn to us.

'Well, now, how are you all? Sit down and get on with your tea. You seem to have plenty to eat. Yes, er well, that's good.' A longish pause. 'Do they have another meal?' he would enquire, turning back to our governess.

'Oh no, my Lord, this is the last meal of the day.'

'Of course, of course. Quite right.'

And with that he would turn on his heel and make good his retreat. As the door shut behind him a great wave of relief would sweep over us and the evening would return to something near normality.

The years slipped by and Eve and I grew up together, a strong bond of affection being forged between us which was to remain throughout our lives. We seemed to spend most of our time at Highclere, but at irregular intervals we would be taken up to stay at our London house at 13 Berkeley Square. This was the house where I had been born on 7 November 1898. It was not large and was mainly used by my parents during the London season when they brought the servants from Highclere with them.

My earliest memories of it make it tall and small and darkly green. Yet I know that when the family were all there the staff consisted of no less than fourteen so they must have all been fitted in somewhere. First there was my father's butler, Streatfield, a great character with mutton-chop whiskers who always spoke in a pedantic fashion. He had a trick of putting aitches where they ought not to be and dropping them where they should have been. 'Yhars, m'Lord,' he used to say, 'heverything is quite hall right.' He was the typical, efficient English butler of that era, gravely deferential and prepared at all times to deal with all exigencies. He was stern but had a fondness for children.

Next there was my father's valet, Fearnside, a remarkably loyal man who handled all my father's personal affairs. Then there was my mother's maid and Roberts, who had the title 'groom of the chambers'. Next came the housekeeper, the cook, two kitchen maids, three housemaids and finally two footmen.

Our London home was retained almost to the end of the First World War and as my grandmother, Marie Wombwell, lived just around the corner at 20 Bruton Street, I saw more of her than of my father and mother who were often abroad. Granny lived a somewhat empty life and I was one of her few sources of consolation; I spent a great deal of time with her and she spoilt me tremendously. Until I was six years of age she spoke nothing but French to me so that I was soon fluent in that tongue.

When I was eight, I went to a private school called Ludgrove in New Barnet, Hertfordshire. Of its kind, it was a very good school indeed, but I did not do anything particularly exciting there except to get my colours at cricket and football. At that time I still thought in French and when I could not remember English words and lapsed into French, I well remember the boys kicking my bottom and calling me 'dirty frog'.

The masters at Ludgrove tried hard to instil Latin and Greek into my head for in those days such subjects were considered most important and it was their job to see that I was correctly prepared by thirteen for entry to public school, which in my case, following family tradition, was to be Eton. I shall not continue to describe life at Ludgrove for I find that the majority of people who write their memoirs devote far too much time to their early youth.

Two incidents of my childhood, however, stand out in my memory. My grandfather, the Fourth Earl, had been one of the finest classical scholars of his generation and when, as

Lord Lieutenant of Ireland, he had given his inaugural oration as Viceroy at Trinity College, Dublin, in Latin, he had admitted, when pressed, that he could as easily have made the speech in Greek. My father, even at the age of ten, would scarcely have been considered backward by present day standards of education, for by then he was bilingual in French and possessed a fair knowledge of German, Latin and the rudiments of Greek. I, alas, enjoyed no such reputation.

Usually when I returned from school – accompanied by a very indifferent report – I would receive a summons to my father's study. He would be sitting at his desk and, as I came in, would look up and say, 'Ah, my dear Porchester . . .' for as you may remember he would only call me Henry if he was in a good mood. 'As usual, your reports are very bad. Your writing is slovenly, your mathematics are appalling, and apparently you don't pay sufficient attention. I am paying for your education to make you a useful citizen in later life, but all you do is to idle your time away, so I have decided to engage a tutor to bring you up to the required standard. His name is Mr Lusk and you'll do three hours' work in the schoolroom each morning, and one hour in the afternoon. Saturday afternoons, of course, you will have off and Sundays likewise. Now you'd better take heed of this warning, Porchester. I expect a distinct improvement, d'you understand? Off you go.' And with that perfunctory statement, he would dismiss me back to the top floor where we children lived, ate, played and slept, using only the back staircase to gain access or make our escape to the outside world.

However, even the tutor's efforts were of little avail and eventually my father decided to take matters into his own hands and sent a message to my tutor to take me along to Wessex bedroom. As I had seen Blake, his head gardener, making three birch rods for my father, I guessed what was about to happen and was desperately frightened when I entered the room and saw the rods tied up with blue ribbon. I was told to undress and my hands were tied down to the brass bedstead. Almost immediately my father came into the room and, ignoring me, went over to the birch rods, picking up each in turn and swishing it through the air until he seemed satisfied with the one he had selected.

'Now Porchester,' he began, 'I'm going to teach you a sharp lesson. I'm just about *sick* of your behaviour and I hope you're going to damn well remember in future that I'm standing no more nonsense from you of any sort. You are expected to work a lot *harder* than you have been doing and altogether to be a much *better* boy in every way than you are shaping at the moment. I am going to give you six of the very best ...'

Standing back he performed a little on-the-spot jig, as if tautening his muscles, and then suddenly brought down the birch as hard as he could on to my bare bum. After the sixth stroke, he threw down the birch and went out of the room.

Lusk, a friendly New Zealander of approximately thirty years of age, was full of concern and took me back to my room where he bathed my bottom in warm water and rubbed in some soothing ointment. 'I'll tell you what,' he said, grinning, 'you'll have to eat your supper standing up, and I think for the next few days you're going to have to sleep face downward on your bed.'

This little episode had, as one might expect, a deep psychological effect upon me which was to last for many years. From that day onwards, I planned to kill my father and when a few weeks later I found him alone practising golf shots, I concealed myself in some bushes nearby in order to observe him, unseen. I had brought with me a little dagger which seemed well fitted to the task in hand. But I was fearful of two things. Firstly, being caught and then, should I succeed, being sent to Borstal. So I forsook the project.

But if I was unpopular with my father, I was no better regarded by my dear mother. An example of my unpopularity occurred a year later when I was a guest, among several hundred children, at a Buckingham Palace garden party given by King Edward VII and his Queen. For this occasion I was wearing for the first time an Eton jacket and top hat.

The chief excitement of the afternoon, so far as the children were concerned, came when a huge paper balloon, floating some two hundred feet above the crowd and designed as an outsize tiger, disgorged from its belly a cascade of toys. Beneath the balloon the gardeners had roped off a large square of ground which all children were forbidden to enter in case any of them might be injured by the descending packages. Determined that at all costs I would be first upon the scene to seize one or two of the most interesting-looking parcels, I stationed myself very near the ropes ready to rush forward.

Unfortunately, my timing was somewhat awry. A huge bang echoed from the balloon and, as I sprang forward, a cloud of packages rained down. I rushed back to regain the safety of the lawn and ran straight into His Majesty's stomach. With a grunt, the King, known popularly as 'Tum Tum', collapsed on to the lawn. Courtiers rushed to help him to his feet and began dusting him down and someone grabbed hold of me. But His Majesty was extremely kind and said in his guttural tongue, 'No, no, don't worry; the poor little fellow was frightened. I am all right, don't worry.'

At that precise moment, by the grace of God, my mother was some distance away but Queen Alexandra, hearing of the incident, hastened to see if her husband had been hurt. She was wearing a long heliotrope dress with a bird-nest hat perched on her head. Later, she described the incident to Vi de Trafford, thus ensuring that the story would eventually be passed to my mother.

I was deeply upset at the enormity of my crime and did not know whether to cry or run for my life when Princess Mary – later the Princess Royal – who had observed the catastrophe, took me into a tent to comfort me with a raspberry ice-cream. She ordered two, passing one to me. I was so agitated that, as I took it, the wretched thing slipped off the plate and slithered right down the front of her white satin dress. The Princess's governess went almost hysterical with rage. 'You careless boy ... you stupid, careless little wretch!' she cried. Paralysed with fear, I watched the Princess being whisked away to change her dress and awaited the wrath I knew was about to come. It was not long descending. My mother appeared, grasped my arm, nearly dislocating my shoulder, and dragged me to the entrance of the Palace where our carriage was waiting. As the royal footman was given our name, his voice boomed out across the courtyard, 'Lady Carnarvon's carriage.' Miserably, I awaited the arrival of our Brougham. Immediately it came I was thrust inside to receive the first instalment of her anger. It was the fashion at that time to wear very pointed shoes and throughout the journey to 13 Berkeley Square, my mother never for a second left off kicking me in the shins. During the performance she punctuated her pent up fury with such expressions as, 'You little beast'–kick–'you disgraceful boy'–kick–'you shamed me today'–kick.

By the time we reached the front door of our house, I was sobbing. Roberts opened the door and one glance at her Ladyship's face was sufficient to convey to him that his mistress was gravely displeased.

'Roberts, you are to take Lord Porchester to the unoccupied room in the attic this instant, throw some blankets on the bed and lock him in. If he wishes to go to the lavatory he will ring the bell and be escorted there and back again. He is to have *nothing* but bread and milk three times a day for forty eight hours. Do exactly as I say.'

'Very well, my Lady. I will see that your Ladyship's instructions are carried out.' As he turned, he caught my eye and gave a surreptitious wink.

As soon as we had ascended the stairs and were well out of earshot, he turned to me and said, 'I am sorry about this, m'Lord, but don't worry too much. Now tell me what happened. We'll have to carry out your mother's instructions, but I'll get hold of your pyjamas and, of course, make up the bed. When I bring you your bread and milk no-one will know, will they, if by accident a few little extras find their way on to the tray?'

Still racked with sobs, I managed to thank him as he left me in the little room.

The following morning two incidents occurred of which I was not to know until later. The first was a note from Princess Mary, enclosing a jade paper knife, saying that she hoped I was not too upset about the accident to her dress. Only an hour or two later, a carriage arrived from Buckingham Palace containing a sack of toys with a personal message from the King saying that he hoped the mishap had not marred my enjoyment of the afternoon. My mother, however, never allowed me to see the toys and they were despatched forthwith to a children's hospital. These two occurrences well illustrate the great gulf between my parents and me and give some insight into the life of an aristocratic family at the turn of the century.

Christmas was another occasion which always emphasized the remoteness of my parents. On Christmas Eve, presents would be delivered to our Nanny for inclusion in our stockings. They were obviously chosen with little care or regard for our personal tastes. We would see nobody but our Nanny and the servants on Christmas Eve or on Christmas morning until after luncheon when we might be sent for to be shown off to the house guests. After about a quarter of an hour my father would say, 'I think you should go out now for a brisk walk before dark and perhaps we shall see you tomorrow.' Thus we were taken away so that the adults could get down to a serious game of cards.

Sometimes my parents might visit the nursery with their guests, but these excursions were dreaded by us rather than welcomed. From this you can see that being sent off to boarding school at an early age was no great shock; although I missed my sister, I was neither lonely nor homesick.

When I was in my last term at Ludgrove, it was suddenly sprung upon me that I was to be a page at the coronation of George v. I now came under the stern gaze of the Earl Marshall of England, the bearded Duke of Norfolk. I had leave from school to stay at our London house so that I could attend the protracted rehearsals in Westminster Abbey, at the end of which the Duke, much to our amusement, used to offer each of us pages a large chocolate filled with delicious white cream if our efforts had satisfied him. After three major rehearsals, we were deemed proficient and all that remained for us was to collect our page's outfits from our tailors.

On the Coronation Day itself, as the guns thundered across Hyde Park and the bells of Westminster pealed out, our world seemed sublime and secure. I gazed upon the serried ranks of resplendent uniforms and ladies bedecked with jewels. One man stood out among the rest and his image has remained for ever locked in my memory. It was Kaiser Wilhelm. But it was not the figure of the man so much as his waxed moustaches, twisted to perfection, which seemed to epitomize the arrogance of the contemporary German. Sad to relate, with the exception of Bunny Romilly, I am the only survivor of the eight pages for the Great War was to scythe through my contemporaries.

From my point of view much the best event which happened to me in 1911, infinitely more fun than being a page, was being given a sixteen-bore, single-barrelled, non-ejector gun by my father. At first I went out on my own accompanied by my father's head keeper, Henry Maber. He was a big, florid man hailing from Norfolk, a true countryman steeped in all the wisdom of his art, who rode a stout cob to enable him to cover the thousands of acres of the estate to supervise the multitudinous duties of the keepers.

Henry Maber's language, while respectful, was colourful and direct. On one particular morning, my father had begun to discuss the placing of the guns when he cut in to say: 'Excuse me, m'Lord. Before you go any further I'd like you to get the lee side of me. Mrs Maber told me my breath didn't smell very sweet this morning.'

In those days, the only thing that counted was the number of head of game shot. To-day it is the quality that matters. Maber knew a lot about rearing pheasants and we could usually hold our own as to the size of our bags. He was well liked by his under-keepers, the estate workers and our guests alike.

On one occasion we were walking up Lime Avenue and had just reached a particular beech when he spotted a young gardener, Digweed by name, who was acting as a stop. However, at that moment he happened to be relieving nature against a tree. 'Now, Digweed,' Maber roared, 'you turnip-headed gardener, stop that there dung-spreeding and keep on tapping.'

As soon as I was considered safe and proficient, I was allowed out with other guns. I remember, as if it were yesterday, the first time I did this. Henry Maber was present, as was my father's physician and close friend, Dr Marcus Johnson. We had crossed the lawn and were just walking through the park when a cock pheasant rose about thirty yards away. I raised my gun and shot him dead.

Not long after, when my father felt that I had become responsible in handling my gun, he allowed me a stand at one of our shooting parties. I was placed on the outside of the Marquis of Ripon. He was a very jealous shot and a very good one who always used hammer guns right up to the end. He turned to me and in his reedy voice, almost approaching a falsetto, said, 'Dear boy, I will give you one shilling for every head of game you shoot to-day.'

'Thank you very much, Lord Ripon, it is most kind of you.'

My father, who was standing nearby, said with a twinkle in his eye, 'Well, dear boy, I hope you shoot something.'

I was put on the outside and in those days there were quite a few rabbits and a lot of pheasants and during the day I managed to shoot thirty-seven head and, in due course, was paid by his Lordship two gold sovereigns, with the gesture that I might keep the change.

However, there was another little incident during the day which depicted the old man's character. At one stand, a cock flew across him at which he fired both barrels and missed. More by luck than skill I managed to kill it but one thing old Ollie loathed was having his eye wiped by anybody, least of all a twelve-year-old boy. Nevertheless, he turned to me and said dryly, 'Well done, dear boy, well done.' But for the rest of the day he shot everything that appeared likely to come anywhere near me!

During these early years, while my enthusiasm for shooting was being kindled, I had much encouragement from all of my father's friends and none more than from my godfather, Prince Victor Duleep Singh, and his brother Freddy, who often visited us. Prince Victor's father, the Maharajah, had married a European and Victor, born in 1866, became a Captain in the Royal Dragoons and was married, in the year of my birth, to Anne, daughter of the Earl of Coventry. For a wedding present, my father had given him a gift of a square-cut sapphire ring: a man's ring for which my father had paid four hundred pounds. Victor very generously left the ring to me in his will and the history of that ring, of exceptional colour and beauty, together with its escalation in value, I shall relate anon.

Victor was a man of huge proportions, always immaculately dressed in spats. He was an excellent shot who had both barrels of his guns full choke and was a joy to watch. I often stood at his side full of admiration at the accuracy of his shooting which enabled him to decapitate low pheasants. On one occasion, at a stand down by the boathouse, with two loaders and three guns he killed one hundred and forty-seven pheasants.

Apart from his two loaders, His Highness would always take along a boy whose job was to carry a wicker seat, into which the Prince would slump, as no ordinary shooting stick could be expected to bear his weight. He was a tremendous eater and I recall a luncheon when he so filled his plate with curried eggs that the sauce overflowed on to the tablecloth. (The late Aga Khan used to do the same thing, but with curried prawns.) My father had put at godfather Victor's disposal a pony cart, rather like a very small phaeton, in order to carry him from stand to stand. Once, as he hoisted himself into the seat after lunch, there was a resounding crack and one of the shafts broke with the burden of his weight. The accident almost dislodged the footman who was sitting in the monkey seat with his arms folded across his chest. Having overcome their initial shock, the whole party roared with laughter.

3
Sandhurst Scenes

Just before the assassination of the Archduke and before the beginning of hostilities in the First World War, Field-Marshal Lord Kitchener came to luncheon with my parents at Highclere. My father had originally met him when the great man was Sirdar in Egypt. At that time my father was digging in the Valley of the Kings with Howard Carter, in an attempt to find the missing tomb of Tutankhamen.

Kitchener's visit was the result of a suggestion by my mother that, in the event of war, Highclere Castle should be turned into a hospital for wounded officers. My father was lukewarm about this but my mother, having discussed it with her 'father' Alfred de Rothschild and obtained his financial support, would not be deterred. When the plan was finally agreed my father, ruefully, turned to K and said, 'In future, my dear K, our telegraphic address will have to be AMPUTATE, HIGHCLERE.'

On this occasion, K was in mufti. Of course, he was every young man's hero and already his picture was appearing in newspapers and on hoardings beckoning all young men to rally to their country's aid. I was still at Eton and so too young, but looking me over, he enquired, 'What do you think you will want to do?'

'Oh, sir, if the war hasn't ended, I should like to join the Army and become a cavalry officer, but at the moment I'm afraid I'm still too young.'

He laughed kindly and said, 'Well, we shall have to see won't we?'

The hospital opened in August 1914 amidst much excitement and bustling activity. Our family physician, Dr Marcus Johnson, was enrolled as medical director and my mother set about finding the best nurses possible. This involved her in frequent visits to New Court, Rothschild's headquarters, and occasionally I accompanied her.

Almina was in the very happy position of being able to go to her father and ask for five, ten or twenty thousand pounds, to which he would gently reply, 'Oh, puss-cat, I gave you ten thousand pounds only last week. Whatever have you done with it, my darling child?'

She would duly explain and Alfred would simply write out another cheque. She was never refused. However, sometimes her father would say, 'Oh my darling, you are terribly extravagant. Do try and be more careful. I know it is all in a very good cause.'

For my part, I remember my visits for equally mercenary reasons. We usually found three Rothschilds sitting at their desks: Nathan, Leo and Alfred were always delighted to see me and very spoiling. I never received less than a ten-pound note from my godfather Alfred and sometimes from Leo as much as ten gold sovereigns, or occasionally a gold five-pound piece. As my father kept me on a very tight rein, these additions to my pocket money were greatly appreciated.

Shortly after the war had got under way, my father's half-brother, Aubrey Herbert, decided that he should enlist. His brother-in-law, Tom de Vesey, was Colonel of the Irish Guards. Unfortunately, no-one could have been more ill-equipped to join the army than dear Aubrey. Untidy, with poor sight, he looked very bizarre in uniform. But he was not to be dissuaded and, as he spoke perfect German, he was duly accepted into the Irish Guards who felt he would be useful as an interpreter. At the time he was Member of Parliament for Yeovil.

Having collected his uniform from his tailor only a few days previously, he was walking in the West End of London when he happened to run into the Provost Marshal, Jim Athlumney, who was a Brigadier-General. As Jim drew nearer he could hardly believe his eyes.

'Aubrey! Good God!'

To this greeting Aubrey managed a half-hearted salute.

'Great Heavens, Aubrey, what on earth are you doing dressed like that? For God's sake jump into a cab and get out of sight,' said the man who was responsible for army discipline in the London District.

'W-what's the matter?' began Aubrey innocently.

Lord Athlumney could hardly contain himself.

'Well, for a start you've only shaved one side of yer face and the soap's still clinging round yer ears and yer collar.'

'Oh dear,' Aubrey replied, 'I'm so sorry – I know I'm absent-minded. I do that occasionally.'

'And your uniform – I've never seen anything like it in all my life. Look at your buttons,' his Lordship continued, 'your *buttons*, and your *trousers* . . . Please never come out like this again because, if you do and I see you, I'm afraid I shall have to arrest you!'

Duly chastened, Aubrey fled.

He was sent to France and his regiment was caught up in the retreat from Mons. During it, he learned that the Colonel, his brother-in-law Tom, had been seriously wounded. Aubrey decided that he'd better ride back and see if he could find him. He, therefore, took the opposite direction to the retreating troops and trotted along towards the enemy. Unfortunately, it was the enemy he found, rather than his brother-in-law.

One bullet hit him just below his heart and hurled him to the ground. In great pain and believing that he was dying, he recalled that he had been issued with three little morphine tablets that he had put in a pillbox in his pocket. Instructed that if badly wounded he should take one of them, he now decided to make a good job of the matter and take all three as he was obviously *in extremis*. This had the effect of rendering him totally unconscious and, undoubtedly, this action was to save his life. With lack of movement, his blood quickly clotted and he remained lying in the same position for almost twelve hours.

In due course the Germans came round to collect the corpses and flung Aubrey with the rest of the cadavers into a small church to await burial the following morning, putting a sentry on the door.

Sometime, in the middle of the night, this man received the fright of his life when he heard a sepulchral voice coming from within. He promptly called out the officer of the guard who was more sceptical than he that a ghost of their victims had already taken possession of the church. Obtaining a lantern, he went in to find Aubrey Herbert, badly wounded but still alive.

When the officer knelt over him he found that the wounded soldier was an Englishman who promptly addressed him in fluent German: 'I've been badly injured. Could you kindly take me to hospital?' The German was shocked, apologized, and explained that all the bodies in the church were believed dead. He immediately arranged for a stretcher and ambulance to convey Aubrey to hospital at Château Thierry. The surgeons operated at once and he received the finest treatment.

At the hospital another piece of good fortune overtook him. The Germans were forced to retreat after the battle of the Marne, and the hospital was overrun by the British. Not only did they find my father's half-brother but a note tied to his bed, written in English, describing exactly the treatment he had been given.

It was not long before he was at Highclere, as a patient this time rather than a house guest. In a bed beside him was George Paynter, an officer in the Scots Guards. He had also been severely wounded, but shortly afterwards, when well on the way to recovery, his roving eye beheld a delicious young, auburn-haired nurse. Everyone seemed to be in love with her and I'm not at all sure that it didn't include me, in spite of the fact that I was still at Eton.

However, my mother, acting as a sort of commander-in-chief-cum-matron, was in the habit of patrolling the Castle at all hours of the day and night. One evening, dressed in uniform and on her rounds, she caught George Paynter *in flagrante delicto* with the beautiful nurse. Always discreet, she retreated from the room and the following morning called the nurse in to see her.

'Look here, my dear, I'm afraid you'll have to go. I cannot have my nurses behaving in this fashion. That sort of thing must put a great strain on the patient's heart and he might well have died as a result.'

Everyone's sweetheart left, much to their sorrow.

Aubrey avoided being invalided out of the army and was eventually sent to the Dardanelles, where he made something of a name for himself. The fact was that he knew the area well and shortly before the war had been approached by the Government of Albania which offered him the throne of that small country. He had immediately cabled my father: 'HAVE BEEN OFFERED THRONE OF ALBANIA STOP MAY I ACCEPT LOVE AUBREY'. The cabled reply he received was terse and to the point: 'NO CARNARVON'.

In the Dardanelles Aubrey became something of a legend. Firstly, he was *persona grata* with the Turks and could speak their language. One day he suddenly decided that it might be a good thing if he were to address the enemy. Consequently, and to everyone's amazement, he climbed on top of the trench and began to harangue them in their own tongue. He explained how stupid they were and how misguided to be fighting the British. This led to immediate fraternization and Aubrey persisted in his tactics until word got back to the GOC. He was promptly ordered to stop talking to the Turks.

Aubrey was in many ways a fantastic man. He always

declared that if the matter had been handled properly, Turkey would never have entered the war against the Allies. He said that in 1914 he was informed that Turkey was prepared to remain neutral if payment was made of six million pounds. So certain was Aubrey of the matter that he went to see Sir Edward Grey, who was at that time the Foreign Secretary. He proposed that if he were given the necessary authority and backing, he would go out and negotiate the terms of their neutrality. To this suggestion Grey replied pompously, 'No, Sir, that is quite impossible. It would be beneath the dignity of His Majesty's Government to even consider negotiations of such a nature.' If such negotiations could have been successfully concluded, there is no knowing how many tens of thousands of lives might have been saved, let alone the Mesopotamian campaign in which I was shortly destined to participate.

By now, as the war advanced, the casualty lists were growing ever longer and daily we looked down the columns in *The Times* to read of the deaths of so many friends and acquaintances.

In due course, although yet still too young, I tackled my father on the subject of doing my share in the war: 'The sooner I can get into Sandhurst the better.'

He replied, 'Well, Henry, if you feel that way, I am not going to discourage you.'

However, there was a very distinct problem: by the end of my career at Eton I had become reasonably proficient in a number of subjects, but unfortunately mathematics was not among them. It was, therefore, decided that I had better go to a crammer in Norfolk to brush up on maths. In due course I took the entrance exam at the Imperial Institute and was told at its conclusion that although I had done quite well in certain subjects, I had failed abysmally in mathematics. No doubt at the mention of Kitchener's name my shortcomings were overlooked. My military career was about to begin.

On arrival at Camberley I was posted to 'C' Company,

the Cavalry Company having recently been disbanded. There was a sense of urgency about the Royal Military Academy but the pattern of life seemed yet unaffected by the terrible losses we were sustaining on the Western Front.

Captain Dalrymple-Hamilton was our adjutant, a very strict man but efficient. The NCOs were terrific, all guardsmen and disciplinarians to their fingertips: they were fair and not without humour.

One Monday morning, after a week-end leave which had involved me in something of a hangover, we mustered on the parade ground. Our drill sergeant strode up and down the ranks, looking at us with a piercing eye. I was feeling none too good at the time and was quite unable to conceal it. Having passed me on several occasions, he suddenly came to a halt and stood staring directly into my blood-shot eyes.

'Lord Porchester, Sir!' he shouted at the top of his voice. 'You look like a wet dream. Pull your bloody self together, Sir!'

This admonition, in front of the entire company, was not without its salutary effect.

We boxed, we swam, we drilled and we learned bayonet fighting on dummies. 'Go on, Lord Porchester, Sir, he's a Hun; stick it in his guts! We've got to beat these buggers, not make love to 'em!'

Among my contemporaries at Sandhurst were Dick McCreery and Miles Dempsey who both became famous names in the Second World War, Lump Altamont, Miles Graham and Harry Kerr, Lord Greville's son, who was my closest friend at Eton. He and so many of them were shortly to die in France, but some survived to do battle in the Second World War. The walls of Eton carry their memorials as do schools all over Britain of former inmates.

My father had agreed to give me an allowance of fifteen pounds a month. I cannot say that I felt particularly flush but life was still gay and, despite the very rigorous course which was to last six months, we still had time to enjoy ourselves. One amusing incident I recall with glee. A pal of mine called

Pilks amused himself one moonlight night climbing to the top of the flag-staff on the main building where he crowned the pole with a standard WDJerry. None of the staff could find out how this object had reached such an exalted position and the adjutant gave orders to one of his picked marksmen – a splendid colour-sergeant in the Brigade of Guards – to shoot down the offending object with a ·22 rifle. It took him about a dozen shots before he eventually smashed it, much to the amusement of the cadets who were watching.

While at Sandhurst I had my first love affair and her name was Modesta. I met her at a party in London and I remember vividly the night when she invited me to her flat at Museum Mansions in Great Russell Street. She was an actress and very pretty. She was also ten years older than I. She had two rooms and a little kitchen, and in the sitting room a large white polar bear rug lay stretched out before the fireplace.

I was all of a tremble as she left me alone for a moment or two saying, 'If you shut those beautiful blue eyes, Porchey dear, I'll soon be with you.'

My heart was thumping like a triphammer and I was paralysed with fear. When she returned she was in a negligée, her hair loosely round her shoulders. In a second she sensed her role and endeavoured to quiet my fears.

She kissed me and gently pulled me down beside her. It was snowing outside.

'Just relax and take off your clothes,' she whispered.

I did as I was bid. It was all cock sparrow stuff, I fear, and over before I knew it.

'Never mind,' she said, 'next time you'll enjoy it far more.'

She was sweet and beautiful, and I was a lucky boy to have met up with such a charmer. When I left her flat, there was a thick carpet of snow on the ground.

Dick Dawson, my father's trainer at Whatcombe, had generously loaned me an old car. This was strictly against regulations, but I managed to garage it at Pytchells and was never found out. On many occasions it transported me to the racecourse, the West End, or other assignments.

I had, of course, very little money and on one occasion I backed a couple of horses which ran very badly and I needed fifty pounds to pay my bookmaker. I wrote to my father explaining my situation and asking him if he would be so kind as to lend me fifty pounds. Two or three days later I received his reply, which read as follows:

My dear Henry,

There is a very old axiom 'if you want money, back horses ... and you will go on wanting.' It also occurred to me to wonder that if you had won, would you have sent *me* fifty pounds? I doubt it. However on this occasion, I will do as you ask, but *never* will it be repeated.

Yours affectionately,
Carnarvon

Enclosed within the letter was a cheque made out *to* my father for the sum of fifty pounds, and signed by one of his friends, T.P.King, but my forgetful father had forgotten to endorse the cheque. Having only just opened a banking account of my own, I was not aware of such requirements and forthwith repaired to my local branch at Camberley. When I presented the cheque, the teller pointed out that he was unable to cash it, due to the fact that it had not been endorsed by my father. Somewhat nonplussed and dispirited, I went back to Sandhurst taking the cheque with me. The post in those days was slow and the thought of returning the cheque to Highclere, where undoubtedly it would receive scant attention, if any, seemed to me a course of action which should be avoided. All the wretched thing required was my father's signature; he, after all, had sent the cheque to me, there was no doubt as to his intentions and so I decided to forge his signature. I obtained a piece of tracing paper, practised his signature and duly endorsed the cheque. This was, of course, an abysmally stupid thing to do, but it didn't seem like that at the time; merely an expedient method by which I could obtain the money quickly. Allowing two days' grace, I duly re-presented the cheque and was paid.

Approximately a month elapsed and then, one Saturday afternoon, Tommy Frost and I decided to go racing at Newbury, both of us in uniform. Suddenly I saw my father outside the weighing room. Pointing him out to my friend and waving, I moved towards him. To my utter astonishment, he cut me dead. I was never so surprised in my life and turned away in amazement.

'Good God! What has happened?' I said to Tommy.

I made off in the direction my father had taken and soon caught him up. When I addressed him, he turned round sternly and with cold eyes that glinted in a most unfriendly manner he said, 'I never thought that I would be the father of a thief.'

For a second or two I could hardly believe my ears and became furious.

'How dare you speak to me like that. What on *earth* are you talking about? ... How dare you say such a thing!'

'Don't you, by God! You stole a cheque ...'

'I never did any such thing. How dare you accuse me ...'

'You stole a cheque of mine for fifty pounds ...'

'I did nothing of the sort. What are you talking about? I asked you for fifty pounds and you wrote me a letter – which luckily I've kept – in which you sent me a cheque for fifty pounds signed by your friend, T.P.King ...'

I saw a look of doubt spread over my father's face and I quickly explained exactly what had happened, including my forging of his signature. For a few long moments there was silence.

'Good God,' he said, 'do you know what I have done ... the awful thing that I have done? I'll never forgive myself. I suspected my valet, George Fearnside, and other servants, and when eventually I found that you had cashed it, I believed you had stolen it.'

Still white hot with anger, I said, 'How dare you think such a thing of me. I know it was very stupid of me to have done what I did with the cheque, but all I was trying to do was to obtain the fifty pounds you had kindly agreed to lend me and I did not think I was doing anything wrong. I'm very sorry.'

My father seemed stunned, staring at me as if hardly comprehending what I was saying, but when he realized the full significance of it, he put out his hand.

'I'm truly sorry, dear boy, I'm most upset. I completely forgot I had sent you the letter. What on earth can I say to Fearnside?'

And with that he turned sorrowfully away.

The summer of 1915 was drifting away, the news from the Western Front bad. We continued our training and discipline was hard. True to the traditions of Sandhurst, not only were they going to turn us into officers but also into men. During our few hours of leave it was not unnatural that we should look for love and laughter. After all, we were young and full of *joie de vivre*.

One day at Lingfield Races, my old friend Atty Persse introduced me to a very pretty girl, an actress called May. She was married to an actor who was the son of one of Edward VII's many paramours at the time he was Prince of Wales. May had a house at Thorn Road, Maidenhead, and also a flat in London as she was working at the time in a play called *Potash and Perlmutter*. We quickly became the greatest of friends and then lovers. She asked me if I could get leave from Sandhurst and come over to lunch at Maidenhead. I got a week-end pass which enabled me to leave Sandhurst about twelve noon on Saturday and I had to be back Sunday evening in time for Mess at eight o'clock. I had arranged with May that I would arrive about one o'clock and she prepared a delicious lunch with a bottle of Moselle on ice.

When I arrived, luckily enough for me, I parked Dick Dawson's old car in the gate-way of a newly mown hay field about one hundred yards from her front door. She let me in and told me that she had sent her servants out until it was time to prepare the evening meal. The doors were locked and, after lunch, at about half-past-two, we hopped into bed.

I was fast asleep when she awoke me about 4.30 p.m. saying 'get into the bathroom and put your clothes on as quickly as you can. My husband is champing at the bit outside the front door, furious that there are no servants to let him in. I shall try and keep him out as long as I can by pretending I am in bed with a bad headache.'

I threw on my uniform without even waiting to do up my shoes. She told me to let myself out of the bathroom window and drop into the geranium bed which was at least twenty feet below. I closed my eyes, let go and rolled over like a shot rabbit. When I had picked myself up, I ran across the lawn, crawled under the rusty wire of the tennis court, scrambled up the railway embankment and was promptly confronted by a ganger and three of his mates who were repairing the railway line. They grasped their pick axes and hemmed me in as it was perfectly obvious that I was trying to escape from *something*.

'Steady on there, young fella; we know who you are!' the ganger began.

'Now, don't you give us no trouble, 'cause if you do, we'll dosh you with this,' and he brandished his pick axe menacingly, 'there's four of us and only one of you'.

This seemed like a nightmare.

'What the hell do you think you're doing? My name's Lord Porchester and I'm a gentleman cadet at Sandhurst, I'll have you know.'

'Go on, you'll be telling us next that you're the Lord Almighty. Don't give us that crap. What you are's a ruddy Hun who has escaped from the POW camp down the road at Bray. We know. Now, don't give us no trouble because we're going to take you back from where you've come.'

'Are you insane? Here's my identity disc, you bloody fools. I tell you I'm Lord Porchester. I'm on a week-end pass from Sandhurst and if you really want to know, I was in the arms of the most beautiful girl in the world when her ruddy husband returned and I had to leap out of her bathroom window. That's why I'm looking so dishevelled. Now please let me go.'

For a moment the plate-layers seemed nonplussed, and there was a long silence as we glowered at each other, until the ganger, turning to the others, said, 'D'you know, fellas, I reckon I believes him. I don't think any ruddy Hun would know how to concoct a story like that. What do you lads say?'

'Tell us more,' they chorused.

'Well,' I said, 'it was only by good luck I didn't break any bones jumping out of her window.'

The foreman cut in again.

'Tell us, little Lord Fauntleroy, was it really worthwhile?'

'Not half,' I said, and, pushing my way between them, ran off down the line, nipped into my car and drove back to Sandhurst where I had to explain to my close friends why my week-end had ended rather abruptly – much to their amusement.

4

Pig-sticking and Polo

After passing out from Sandhurst, I was gazetted to the 7th Queens Own Hussars and went over to Ireland to join the training regiment which was stationed at Newbridge not far from the Curragh. I spent four months in Ireland, and then received orders to embark on the troop carrier *Nestor*. We sailed on Boxing Day 1916, in convoy on the long journey round the Cape to land finally in Bombay. During the voyage we had several scares from enemy submarines and, on one occasion, I was the orderly officer of the day. Down in the bowels of the ship there were thirty-seven desperate men – all of them Australians – who were being sent back to Australia to be tried for various serious offences, such as desertion in the face of the enemy, and they really were a terrifying bunch. I was accompanied, as always, by two armed Military Policemen and an NCO and I was greeted with catcalls. 'Let us up for some air,' they shouted and became very threatening as they did not feel happy at the possibility of being hit by a torpedo and drowned like rats.

When I arrived at Bombay, I was greeted by Nigs Freeman Thomas who was ADC to Sir George Lloyd, then Governor of Bombay, and bidden to dinner there where I spent one night before joining my regiment at Meerut. Charles Norton was our CO and Roger Evans his Adjutant. I was posted to 'B' Squadron, commanded by Tommy Thornton, at whose wedding to Maudie Fraser, the beautiful daughter of the British Resident in Kashmir, I was shortly to be best man. I am happy to say Tommy is still hale and hearty and remains one of my best friends.

At Meerut I found my regiment established at Gillespie Barracks in the British cavalry lines. Although not modern, the barracks were pleasant and the cantonment had a gracious old-world atmosphere with The Mall flanked by great trees. There were five first-class polo grounds, a racecourse and excellent pig-sticking country in the Kadir, with plenty of snipe and duck close at hand.

Time in India seemed to be standing still. The changing pattern of warfare on the Western Front had little significance in the sun-drenched plains of India. Here the cavalryman still ruled supreme and the Indian Army trained and drilled remorselessly to a pattern that had varied very little during the past two hundred years. As was to be expected any cavalry regiment demanded and obtained a very high standard of horsemanship and skill-at-arms. We young officers spent hour upon hour on equestrian training and sword-play exercise. Dummies would be placed in every conceivable position to be run through with deadly accuracy. There would also be mounted combat between men armed with sabres or lances. There was revolver practice, tent-pegging and pig-sticking, polo and racing, all conceived and played to one ultimate objective – a supreme harmony between horse and man. Only by constant practice could it be achieved, so that whatever the confusion on the field of battle, the roar of the guns, the smoke and the screams of the dying, the soldier and his mount would act as one.

Life in the regiment made no concession to wartime. It was Mess kit each evening and dining off silver plate. We drank the health of the King and the pages of my boyhood reading came alive with every new experience. Our style of life was truly superb.

Each bachelor cavalry officer had five indoor servants: a dogboy to keep his dog free from ticks, to help with the kit cleaning, to frighten away snakes and to walk before his master at night with a hurricane lamp; a man to sweep, clean and empty the latrine; a boy to fetch and carry water and prepare the morning and evening bath; a butler to stand behind his master's chair at meals to see he had everything he wanted; and a bearer responsible for cleaning and pressing the mountains of kit. All lived within the compound together with their wives and families and in addition there were, of course, grooms, stable boys and all their relations too.

This may sound amazing to-day, but remember there was no running water available and no air-conditioning. I might have to change my clothes four or five times a day from undress uniform of blue frock coat and overalls to field service dress of serge, drill breeches and overalls to polo or hunting kit. Then there was also Mess-dress and full-dress uniform. Each of these had its own helmet, cap, boots, spurs belt, sword sling and other accoutrements and each had its equivalent in white linen. Camp kit, guns, swords and revolvers also had to be looked after.

On one splendid occasion, I was fortunate enough to be invited to spend a week-end with the Commander-in-Chief, India, Sir Charles Munro. He was a charming man but his wife was a rather extraordinary woman. At breakfast, on the day of my departure, I witnessed an amazing domestic scene. Lady Munro playfully plucked a very ripe mango from a bowl of fruit on the table and hurled it at Sir Charles's head. For a subaltern to observe such treatment of his Commander-in-Chief was somewhat embarrassing although quite amusing. Sir Charles, a very handsome man with a grey moustache, jerked his head to one side so that the mango swept past him and burst, with a horrible squelch, on a portrait of the Queen.

'My dear, what on earth are you doing? You've gone quite

mad,' and then he covered up the incident with deep chuckling laughter.

The servants leapt into action, the painting was removed and cleaned and the incident forgotten.

Such an occurrence was a relief from the frustrations of regimental life. The war was at its height but all we did was train and train and train, seemingly destined never to get sight nor sound of any enemy. Bad news percolated back from Mesopotamia but still we were not called upon.

The Middle-eastern situation at that time centred round British and Allied attempts to protect the Anglo-Persian oilfields and particularly the refinery at Abadan after Turkey had sided with Germany at the outbreak of war. Not only was it imperative to defend our commercial interests but, in addition, the Royal Navy relied on this source of fuel oil to maintain her presence in the Indian Ocean. By the end of 1914 Turkish cruisers had bombarded Russian ports in the Black Sea and so Russia had declared war on Turkey. On 5 November 1914 France and Britain had done likewise.

Britain had then sent an expedition under the command of General Nixon, an Indian cavalryman, into Mesopotamia. A vigorous and powerful military leader, he struck hard and fast at the low calibre Turkish troops, and with brilliant improvisation captured the Bastra *vilayet* and began to advance up the river Tigris in the general direction of Baghdad, the capital of what is now Iraq. With his army desperately under-strength, fighting in arid and hostile conditions with ever increasing lines of communication, his original and brilliant successes began to be counteracted by stiffening opposition from a stubborn and efficient enemy.

The 14th Hussars had been sent as reinforcements, but the situation began to deteriorate rapidly and some indication as to the extent of the military commitment may be judged by the fact that eventually we were to suffer some forty thousand casualties with the final ignominy that General Townsend, Commander of the 6th Indian Division, who just previously had brilliantly captured Kut and advanced beyond, was finally forced to retreat back to that city which the counter-attacking Turks bypassed in their offensive. In the end, having suffered almost intolerable hardship in intense heat with no food and dwindling ammunition, General Townsend and nine thousand British and Indian soldiers were forced to lay down their arms and surrender.

Not long after came the news of the sinking of HMS *Hampshire* and with it the death by drowning of Lord Kitchener. Add to this the costly but inconclusive battle of Jutland and the terrible losses being inflicted on the Western Front, and the degree of pent up frustration experienced by the 7th Hussars can be judged as they continued their training.

Gradually we were re-equipped with more modern arms and began adapting cavalry tactics to take advantage of our new-found fire-power. No longer would sword rule the day. Mobility, surprise, maximum fire-power from directions not expected by the enemy were to be, Colonel Norton believed, the future role of the cavalry. The Colonel was in the midst of re-organizing us when he was given a brigade in Mesopotamia – but without us. Gloom in the regiment was great when it was learnt that we were all to remain behind in India. Amidst such despondency I was glad when ten days' leave came up enabling me to get away. Off I went to Kashmir to stay with the Maharajah, Hari Singh.

I found the beauty of the country breathtaking with the backdrop of the Himalayas, their peaks capped by the eternal snows, glistening white in the clear blue sky under a brilliant sun. The valleys were filled with lakes, their floating gardens, houseboats and picturesque waterside communities lending an air of enchantment to the scene.

The Maharajah was a wonderful host in every sense of the word and suggested that I should have my own quarters on one of his delightful house-boats on the Dal Lake, not far from Srinagar. He suggested that the first night we should have a western style dinner, just the same type of meal that we would have had at Maxim's in Paris. Sure enough, his

French chef produced a most delightful dinner with lots of champagne and we all went to bed very happy.

We were told to be ready for the big duck shoot which was to start with the morning flight at 5 a.m. There were about twelve guns and when the head keeper blew a whistle, the beaters put up probably anything between two and three thousand duck and they circled around and everybody shot until their guns were hot, which took about twenty minutes. The whistle blew again and a cease-fire took place while the birds that had been shot were picked up. We then had a hearty breakfast, got back into our butts and the second shoot started at about 10 a.m. The same procedure was gone through and we then went back to lunch and either played polo in the afternoon or rested until dinner.

That night my host said he would give us a real Indian feast and we sat on the floor – he dressed in his jewelled turban and flowing robes. I cannot say that I enjoyed that dinner as much as the previous evening but there was quite an amusing sequel. Hari Singh told me that he would send one of his favourite girl-friends, called Little Lotus, down to my house-boat. She was eighteen years old and he said I would find her quite enchanting. When I got back to the boat there was no sign of her. I undressed and went to my cabin all ready to sleep when there was a knock on the door and the lotus flower appeared. She could not speak a word of English and, to my horror, she was chewing betel nut. She was certainly a very pretty girl but I was so put off by the smell of the betel nut that I thanked her politely and, mostly in sign language, explained that I did not want her in my bed. She withdrew immediately and the only person who seemed at all put out was my host who said next day he could not understand why I did not fancy his charming protégé.

On the following day, I went with His Highness's chief *shikari* to try and shoot a big bear. It was a very stiff climb for me and when I did eventually see this huge bear – which normally I could not very well have missed – my hands were shaking so much that when I fired the rifle I not only missed the bear but fell back into the arms of the waiting *shikari*, who was extremely peeved that I had not bagged such a splendid specimen. Later in the morning, I shot a much smaller black bear which happened to be eating ripe mulberries at the top of a tree. I had the skin for years in my study until it was eventually worn away by my dogs lying on it in front of the fire.

My ten days' leave was soon over and I returned to Meerut to find the regiment a-buzz with excitement. As I walked into the orderly room, I saw the short, spindly silhouette of our regimental sergeant-major, Mr Welch. He was a splendid man of Boer War vintage, a disciplinarian to his fingertips. He was addressing one of his clerks in his stentorian voice.

'Now lad,' he said, 'you can start sharpening your sword. We're off at long last. It'll be in orders to-night. Thank God we can stop all this dithering about. We're going to Mespot to see some real fighting. Damn good job too.'

'Not much good my going, Mr Welch. I'm only a third class shot.'

For a moment the RSM was nonplussed, but not for long. 'Well,' he said, 'I'll tell you what, lad. You'll make a damn good target for one as can shoot.'

5
Mesopotamia

Although the telegram which had been received from Army headquarters at Simla had brought joy to the hearts of the regiment when it arrived at 2 a.m. on the morning of 4 October 1917, it had come at a most inopportune moment.

The adjutant, Captain Evans (who was to attain the rank of major-general and was to write an excellent account of this campaign in *The Years Between*), had just completed his three-year tour of duty and had gone back to Staff College at Quetta; his successor, Lieutenant Stevens, had not yet arrived; Colonel Norton had recently been succeeded in command by Major Dalgety, known to each and everyone as Dougald; the orderly room sergeant was down with fever; the quartermaster was about to be medically repatriated and the regimental quartermaster-sergeant had recently received a commission and was now in command of a troop. But the enthusiasm of both officers and men remained unabated.

We were given a general picture of the Mesopotamian situation. The defeat of General Townsend had had a salutary effect upon His Majesty's Government; only five thousand men had originally been sent out in 1914 but by December 1916 General Sir Stanley Maude had assembled an army of two hundred thousand men and seventy-three thousand animals, all re-equipped and fully supplied. Maude had then opened his offensive which, in spite of stubborn defence by the Turks, swung forward through the difficult terrain and shocking climatic conditions. After a series of battles, and not without some misgivings from the War Office, he attacked and entered the capital, Baghdad, on 11 March 1917.

But the Turks were not done yet, and Maude spent the next six months establishing forward defences on the three lines by which the enemy could move through the desert. They were the three rivers Diyala, Tigris and Euphrates. In addition, he also strengthened his lines of communication to Basra, some four hundred miles to the south at the mouth of the river Tigris.

But it was in the early autumn that Intelligence reports, percolating in from behind the Turkish lines, advised the High Command that the enemy were preparing a strong counter-offensive. These reports indicated that they would endeavour to thrust down the line of the Euphrates. It was for this reason that Maude had requested further reinforcements, especially mobile units that could move swiftly across the difficult desert ground to probe the strength of the enemy positions.

Thus on 11 November 1917, GHQ Baghdad had been authorized to form an additional cavalry brigade – the 11th Indian Cavalry Brigade – consisting of the 7th Queen's Own Hussars, Guides Cavalry, 23rd Cavalry and 'W' Battery RHA. This brigade was put under the command of Brigadier-General R.A.Cassels, DSO.

Twelve days later the three troop ships *Rohilla*, *Baroda* and *Egra* carried the 7th Queen's Own Hussars slowly up the Shatt-al-Arab to Basra where horses and men were quickly disembarked and left for the transit camp at Gurmat Ali. By nightfall the following day we were bedded down in our temporary quarters, and were fast recovering from the effects of the sea voyage. However, we immediately began to suffer from the terrible heat. Having longed so heartily to get into action, the morale of the men became somewhat impaired by the aridity of the desert landscape. The news that General Sir Stanley Maude, the victor of Baghdad, had quite suddenly died, gave rise to numerous rumours. Had he been poisoned? How would it affect the future campaign? We need not have worried. Army Headquarters sent orders that when we were ready we should immediately begin the long trek to Baghdad.

Some idea as to the stupefying effect of the heat at Basra may be judged from the fact that, just before our arrival, the British Army lost almost three hundred and sixty men by death from heatstroke. At one point, during the height of the mid-day sun, the wet and dry bulbs on the barometer and thermometers were within one degree of coinciding. If they had done so, all human life would have become extinct, because the temperature of the blood inside the body would have equalled the air outside. Fortunately, our regiment was blessed with an absolutely first-class Irish medical officer whose name was Captain Pettit. Later he was to win a Military Cross. In his rich Irish brogue he counselled everyone as follows: 'There's only one hope for you, boys. I want each man to take off all his clothes and get inside his tent. Soak your towel, socks or anything else and lie down with them placed on your foreheads. Keep your heads moist and drink as much plain water as you want, but only plain water. In that way you should be all right. So, lie down, don't move and stay calm.'

With temperatures soaring between the one-hundred-and-fifteen and the one-hundred-and-twenty mark, his advice was taken to a man and we only lost three from heatstroke. It was almost impossible to draw breath and one found one's lungs gasping for air, but we survived and, having loaded our barges with fodder, began the march north at dawn on 6 December 1917.

Whereas the distance was four hundred miles as the crow flies, we would have to cover a good five hundred miles or more. From Basra to Baghdad the river meandered across a vast flat plain which, in those days, seemed devoid of life or food supplies so we would have to march from supply dump to forage depot, from well to waterhole, skirting the river's bends and twists as best we could.

Each man rode his horse carrying full equipment of sword, rifle, one hundred and twenty rounds of ammunition, cloak and groundsheet, shaving and washing kit, water bottle and canvas bucket, two blankets, picketing pegs and ropes, spare horseshoes and some food for horse and rider. All additional baggage, rations, tents and equipment were carried by mule cart. But these carts were slow and cumbersome and often did not reach the night's camping site until long after dark. Only when they arrived could we bivouac and eat hot bully beef curry or whatever. Then it was up again early in the cool of the morning, water the horses, saddle up, break camp and on to the next waterhole. At mid-day a further long halt was called in whatever shade could be found. We washed down cold bully beef and weevily biscuit with curious-tasting char made with local brackish water, mixed with tinned milk and sugar if we had any. Then full speed ahead to the night's camping place to get all laid out in readiness for everyone else's arrival.

On and on we marched across the arid wastes, during the day in stifling heat but at night experiencing extreme cold, to such an extent that we would even find a thin layer of ice on the canvas water buckets in the morning.

Early one day, as I was inspecting my troop, I glanced across the desert and noticed a huge flock of wild geese at a range of between four and five hundred yards. It occurred to me that, if we could get at them, we might enjoy a welcome change of diet. I estimated that there were two or three hundred of them and they were packed close together, presenting a pretty good target. I popped back to my squadron leader, Alan Breitmeyer, and made a suggestion.

'If we were to send a message back to the Colonel, he could send up "W" Battery and, if they were to load with shrapnel, we might manage to bag some of these geese.'

'Good idea, Porchey. I'll see what the Colonel says.'

He agreed and, in due course, Maclewain, commanding 'W' Battery, came up with four guns. After consultation, it was decided that the first gun should fire over open sights at zero range while the second would put up their sights to one hundred yards and the third and fourth an extra couple of hundred yards between them. The prospect of fresh goose for dinner, a bird I personally do not like eating, had every man craning his eyes to watch the effect of the shoot.

Maclewain decided that all four guns should fire together. Suddenly, with a mighty roar, they blasted flame and smoke. Mounting our horses, we rode forward to collect the victims. Much to Mac's astonishment, there were precisely sixteen birds dead and eight wounded. He was sorely disappointed, considering they had done no better than any self-respecting punt-gunner might expect.

'Old Johnny Turk ain't got nothin' to fear,' came one laconic complaint from a trooper. But there was enough meat on the birds for every trooper in the squadron to have goose for dinner that night.

Soon we arrived at Qurna, which is reputed to be the site of the Garden of Eden. Anything less like a garden would be difficult to imagine; but amidst the thorn scrub was one gnarled remnant of a tree which, traditionally, is recognized as the Tree of Knowledge.

Ever onwards the column marched, cutting corners wherever possible at the bends of the river, kicking up dust swirls from the horses' hoofs until we passed Ezra's tomb and the Shrine of the Prophet, standing black amidst a collection of palms.

As we moved steadily north we became aware of greater activity around us. Arabs appeared to be prowling our camps at night and we feared that they were after our rifles. Normally each trooper slept with his rifle buried in a shallow pit underneath him but one squadron felt lazy one night and safeguarded their rifles by running a stout cord through the trigger guards and making the ends fast to their tent poles. In the morning eleven were missing. Not all were recovered but a few turned up in a nearby Arab village hidden in the granary.

At Sheikh Shi we were deluged by torrential downpours of rain. Within hours the desert was turned into a sea of mud, to such effect that it was almost impossible to move the horses down to their watering points. Conditions were so bad that no further advance could be made for seven days. The temperature fell and although we got some mail at Christmas, there was little cheer and we could only wait for a break in the weather. We were able to move on Boxing Day and by New Year's Day had reached the scene of the most bitter fighting during General Maude's campaign. In due course we reached Kut, the site of Townsend's surrender, and camped amidst the forlorn debris of his gallant defence against the Turks. Old trenches, barbed wire, broken carts gave the area a sense of desolation. That night, before we bivouacked, Alan Breitmeyer made a suggestion.

'I say, Porchey, it might be rather fun if we went out with our guns and sat in some of those disused Turkish trenches about a mile away from here. With a bit of luck, we should get a shot at an evening flight of duck, or pick up another goose or two. But if the worst comes to the worst, I suppose we will be certain to find sand grouse. Anyway, how about it?'

'Love to,' I replied and after the tents had been pitched and the troops settled down, we set off, I taking my servant, Trooper Mackland, and Brit taking his trumpeter, whose name was Marshall. It was half an hour before sunset and by great good fortune, I had either forgotten or neglected to change my military saddle, which I would normally have done, and dangling from it was my Wilkinson sword. Brit had changed his while our two men had put our guns in their rifle buckets.

About two or three miles from camp we saw a long line of Turkish trenches and Brit reined in his horse.

'Look, Porchey, I don't know what you think, but this seems as good a place as any. I think I shall get into that trench over there and if you drop down a hundred yards over to the right we'll see what happens. Is that okay?'

'Sure,' I replied, and off we went.

I was riding a very nice black country-bred horse called Sausage and had noticed that on the far side of the trenches there was a little short *wadi*, in which the animals could be put and remain unseen. This meant the horses must cross the trenches which provided a simple and inviting little jump. I gathered up Sausage, he leapt cleanly into the air but as his forefeet landed on the revetment on the far side, it suddenly crumbled with his weight and began to collapse into the trench. The horse struggled for a moment, lost his balance and keeled over, taking me down underneath him.

For a moment I seemed to lose consciousness, having been transported in one fell moment from bright sunlight to the inky blackness of a well. As I regained my senses, I felt the vast weight of the horse crushing my face into the sand. After some spasmodic kicks, the horse instinctively knew it was defeated and mercifully remained still. Amazingly my life was being saved by the resilience and fine temper of my sword. This, in my fall, had somehow wedged itself under Sausage and on it the full weight of the horse was now resting.

Within seconds I could hear the anxious voice of Brit calling down to me.

'Are you all right? Quick, Mackland, lend me a hand.'

Sausage began to struggle again and Breitmeyer, realizing the peril, grasped the horse's head in a vice-like grip and drew his pistol.

'Marshall!' he yelled at the top of his voice, 'get mounted and gallop back to camp, we cannot possibly pull the horse out alone. Bring back twelve men at least with as many picketing ropes as you can lay your hands on and get back fast!'

In a fresh slither of rock, stone and sand, my servant dropped down beside me, scooping the rubble away from my nose.

'Are you all right?' he asked, but at first I was unable to

reply being quite incapable of speech. 'Hang on, Sir, hang on. The squadron leader's sent for help, it won't be long in coming.'

Looking round, he tried to find some stakes with which to help shore up the horse's body. But now Breitmeyer needed help to hold down the horse, his own strength ebbing with the exertion. Scrambling up to Breitmeyer, Mackland found the squadron leader, one arm locked round the horse's neck, the other holding his pistol to its head.

'Give me a hand, I don't want to kill the horse; his dead weight could prove fatal.'

For what seemed like eternity, I lay squashed beneath Sausage while Marshall took the three miles return to camp at an extended gallop, raised the alarm and then led the rescue party back. With the help of trenching tools, picketing ropes and the combined heaving of about twenty men, the animal was carefully and cleverly extricated, while two troopers helped protect me from further injury, their shoulders heaving against the horse's body. They had managed to pass me a few sips of water from their water-bottles and suddenly the ordeal was over.

Miraculously, being young and supple, no bones were broken, but in later years X-rays revealed that my spine had become twisted like a corkscrew. Bruised, battered, but otherwise unhurt, I was put aboard another horse and we walked slowly back to camp. Sausage had also escaped uninjured. The Wilkinson sword had bent almost double but in so doing had given me a three inch gap with which to survive. I still have that sword to this day.

My penchant for lucky escapes was to continue, for a little over a week later, Brit and I again decided to take our guns and try and bag something for the pot. With four or five troopers acting as beaters, we stood three or four hundred yards from an Arab village. Suddenly, I heard fierce barking and turned round just in time to see a huge Pyard dog, its lips flecked with foam, bounding straight at me. Fortunately, I kept my head, waited until it was ten feet away and shot it with my choke barrel. At the sound of the shot, a black partridge flew over me which I killed with the right barrel.

Breitmeyer, who was a few yards away, had seen the entire show and shouted, 'I think that's the most remarkable right and left that you will ever accomplish!'

We examined the dog from whose path I had leapt and judged that it was rabid.

For ten days we continued until the regiment passed through Ctesiphon, crossed the Diyala river by a bridge of boats until, on 24 January, we camped at Hinaidi on the outskirts of Baghdad. The journey from Basra had been accomplished in twenty-seven marching days, a distance of approximately five hundred miles. A real feat of endurance by man and horse through the shocking weather conditions they had encountered. A few hours later, two enemy planes appeared and dropped a small stick of bombs. Our war had started.

It was some three or four days later, when I had just begun to recover from the strain of our march, that I received an order which stunned me. It was explicit and to the point: 'At dawn, an execution squad of ten men under the command of Second-Lieutenant Lord Porchester will carry out the death sentence on a Turkish officer convicted by general court martial of spying.'

It was my friend Prothero who confidentially imparted the news. 'Terribly sorry about this, Porchey; beastly business; but someone has to do it and your name was drawn from the hat.'

'My God ... I don't think I can ...'

'I know. Look, you'd better have a word with the RSM. He will give you the details and the words of command. It is to be at the West Wall at 0700 hours tomorrow morning. You won't see the man beforehand and a fatigue party will have already prepared the grave. Go and see the RSM.'

It was one of the longest nights of my life. At six o'clock my servant came to awaken me, but I was already up, mechanically preparing myself for the ordeal. How, I wondered, was the victim feeling at this moment? I felt sick.

Having completed my toilet, I walked out from my tent. I could hear the distant sound of the Imam. Perhaps the condemned man's religion would give him comfort. In the distance, innumerable cocks were crowing and I thought of my religion. Offered some breakfast, I declined.

Time was running out. My troop sergeant called me and I walked across to the truck, already loaded with the men. I climbed up beside the driver, the vehicle lurched forward and we began our journey to the western gate. The day was clear and the sun, already creeping above the horizon, was casting dark shadows from the palms, motionless in the stillness of the morning air.

We rounded a corner and I felt sick to my stomach. There, before my eyes, were the awesome details; three or four military policemen, a grave already dug some twenty feet to one side and a wooden post standing five feet from the wall. Before it was the young Turkish officer, not much older than myself. The red caps were completing the business of trussing his legs to the base of the post, his hands were already tied. He was holding his head up and displayed no sign of fear.

I braced myself and, as the truck drew to a halt, jumped out. My troop sergeant intuitively took the lead, calling for the rifles. He took it upon himself to load them – eight live rounds and two blanks. He did it to one side, away from the gaze of the men. The rattle of the bolts brought the expected reaction from the condemned man who, as a trained soldier, recognized the stern implication.

I had been instructed to see that the prisoner's eyes were blindfolded; over his heart I was to pin a white cardboard disc, at which the troopers would aim. When the squad took up arms, I was to draw my sword and the moment I lowered the point the men would fire in unison. Thus the prisoner would not hear the word of command. Immediately after the execution, I was to step forward and with my 38 pistol give him, if necessary, the *coup de grâce*. The thought appalled me.

But first I was expected to ask if he had one last request. In fact, I had been told that he spoke no English but was fluent in French; perhaps this was the reason my name had conveniently come out of the hat! Realizing that any show of weakness on my part would only make it harder for both the victim and the firing squad, I set about my business.

'*M'sieur*,' I began.

'*Bonjour, Lieutenant*,' he replied with an equally firm voice. I chose my French phrases carefully.

'It is my duty to ask you if you have any last request . . .?'

'*Oui, m'sieur*,' he replied quietly, 'may I have a cigarette and please do not bandage my eyes.'

With trembling hands I placed a cigarette between his lips and lit it. His face was ashen now. From the corner of my eye I saw that my troop sergeant had arranged the men behind their rifles, which were lying on the ground. No man would know whether or not his rifle contained a blank but each, no doubt, prayed that it did.

Realizing that further delay was horrible for all concerned, I gave the order to fire. Not daring to look directly, out of the corner of my eye I saw the body twist with the lacerating impact of the bullets and lurch, restrained by the ropes, then slip a few inches, inanimate. One glance told me that their aim had been true. Within seconds I told my squad to get back in the truck. 'Thank God that's over,' I said to them. Ten minutes later we were back in camp.

There were two more incidents I was to witness before our regiment moved forward into action, and both of them were equally harrowing. It is possible that I may well have been the last man in the British Army to have taken part in another barbaric custom long since discontinued: Number One Field Punishment – the cat-o'-nine-tails.

The circumstances were as follows: again our camp had been a focal point for Arab thieving, with the result that two troopers had awakened one morning to find that their weapons had been stolen as they had neglected to secure them in the manner prescribed. They were duly court martialled and both of them were awarded Number One Field Punishment – twenty-five lashes apiece. In this day and age the punishment might seem excessive, but with each rifle stolen there was the increased possibility of British soldiers being killed.

Once again it had fallen to my lot to see the sentence of the court carried out. The flogging was to be administered by two military police with a corporal counting the strokes. The two sentenced men were stripped and the first was brought forward to have his hands lashed to the limber of a gun carriage. The two MPs marched forward with the cat-o'-nine-tails at the high port. I read out the sentence of the court; our medical officer stood by and when I had finished, the corporal of the military police barked, 'Commence punishment!' The two MPs stood on either side of the trooper. Upon the given word of command, the corporal shouted, 'One!' and the cat came down – wham – across the bare flesh of the man's back. 'Two!' and down came the leather thongs once again.

I stood there watching this spectacle, trying not to flinch, marvelling that the trooper concerned made not a sound nor a whimper. After the twenty-fifth stroke, he was cut down and collapsed. The MO stepped forward.

'Now look here, m'boy, I'm going to rub some antiseptic ointment into your back; it'll do you a power of good and stop the risk of infection. It'll sting, mind, but hold on and grit your teeth.'

'Thank you, sir,' came the reply. When the doctor had finished, the soldier stood up straight and asked, 'Permission to leave, sir?'

'Granted,' I replied, and he walked away.

The second trooper, who had had to witness the first performance, was not made of the same fibre. At the very first stroke, he screamed and continued to scream throughout.

Not a word was spoken and I detected, or rather thought I detected, that the two military policemen fractionally increased the severity of their blows, as if marking their displeasure. When the doctor stepped forward to anoint his back, the man screamed at him not to touch it and evoked the response, 'Pull yourself together and no reporting sick in the morning. Off you go.'

It is a sobering thought to reflect that when Queen Victoria's father, the Duke of Kent, was Governor of Gibraltar, he never gave sentences of less than one hundred lashes with a cat-o'-nine-tails, and these for the most trivial offences such as unpolished buttons or late on parade. Such was military discipline a hundred years ago.

The second alarming incident occurred some time later when we were camped on the banks of the Euphrates. A party of about eight men were bathing and one of them – a gunner from 'W' Battery, RHA – was considerably further from the shore than the rest. I was sitting in my tent at the time when the most horrifying screams rent the air. Rushing outside, I could see one of the men flailing the water in agony, while the others endeavoured to drag him to the shore. I ran down to the water's edge and noticed the flow of blood staining the muddy water.

'A bloody shark, sir!' one man shouted. They dragged him ashore and laid him on a towel. One glance was enough; his leg had been torn off at the thigh. Racing up the bank, I found the MO who ran back with me at the double.

'The poor boy will be dead within the hour,' said the MO, 'there's nothing I can do to save him. I shall pump him full of morphine and he shouldn't have much pain. It's a terrible wound, the worst I've ever seen!'

Twenty minutes later the man was dead.

6
Baptism of Fire

Our new Brigade Commander was Brigadier-General Robert Cassels, DSO. He it was who realized the advantage of using cavalry in this terrain, although in other theatres of war the death knell had been tolled for the combination of man and horse as a fighting unit. Whereas the day of drawn swords, the lance and charge had now virtually disappeared, in desert conditions there was still an exceptional role for the cavalry.

During the last four years, the pattern of battle in Mesopotamia had been for the armies to cling to the river banks, using them as an axis for advance or retreat; for both men and animals required water and the deserts on either side were waterless. Cassels, however, believed that the cavalry should strike deep into the desert, by-pass the enemy and savage its rear flank or, better still, its distant lines of communication. By picking their ground carefully, the unit commanders could employ their new-found fire-power to lethal effect. With the use of spotter aircraft, the cavalry could be guided with deft precision to the weakest points of the enemy's defences.

The Turks, for their part, were known to be organizing their own rapid striking force, the Yilderin, or Lightning

Stroke Army, which it was believed they would hurl down the banks of the Euphrates against us.

After eight or nine weeks of further intensive training, a cover story was issued to the men as to the reasons why the regiment was crossing the Tigris by the pontoon near Iron Bridge, which carried the Baghdad–Feluja road to the Euphrates, and they were instructed to divest themselves of all baggage except their essential fighting order. But it was not until 22 March that the 11th Indian Cavalry Brigade, with the 7th Hussars leading, learnt that they were about to take part in a major offensive against the Turks under General Brooking.

The enemy had already withdrawn from Hit to Khan Baghdadi, some forty miles further up the river, and the General intended to move his troops around the enemy's desert lines. Full moonlight was needed for this attack which was to take place on the night of 26–27 March and the cavalry were to advance to Ramadi, ready for operations to begin. At this critical moment, our CO, Colonel Dalgety, was struck down with a high temperature and had to be sent back to hospital and Major Paget-Tomlinson took command. We were to arrive at Sahiliya before dawn on the 25th, and to rest that day prior to going into battle before dawn on the 26th. This meant a march of about fifty miles. A devastating hurricane delayed us at Uqbah, where we rested and watered the animals and this entailed a cold, night-long march of twenty-five miles at a walk. It was dawn on arrival at Sahiliya and as no aeroplanes were sighted, we hoped we had reached the concentration point unobserved.

The enemy position at Khan Baghdadi was about twenty-two miles upstream of Sahiliya. The Turkish 50th Division of 2,800 rifles, twelve to sixteen guns and 150 sabres was entrenched across the main Turkish line of communication, the Khan Baghdadi–Aleppo road, its right flank back in the desert and the left on the Euphrates which was unfordable. Fifteen miles further up the river, the Turks had a further

1,400 rifles, five guns and fifty sabres, with a small garrison still further upstream at Ana.

General Brooking intended to destroy the enemy, whether they stood to fight it out or run for it. On arrival of the cavalry at Sahiliya, he briefed his subordinate commanders. The infantry and artillery would move forward under cover of darkness to attack at dawn, pinning the enemy down, while we, the mobile troops under Cassels, made a wide movement round their desert flank to endeavour to cut their line of retreat up the Aleppo Road. As long rough marching would be entailed, kit and equipment were reduced to a minimum and when we moved on the next day, officers and men each carried only a tin of bully beef, a pocketful of biscuits and a water bottle.

Reveille was to be at 1.30 a.m. and the troops had got their heads down at dusk. Before I turned in, I decided to make a quick tour of inspection. In the cavalry there is only one rule for officers: watch over the welfare of your horses first, your men second and yourself last. I wandered down the lines. Was it my imagination, or did the horses seem fretful? Tossing their heads in the air and sniffing the wind, stamping their feet, were they aware of impending battle? I gave my charger a handful of dates and as usual he spat out the stones with precision. I made a quick check of my troop and then turned in.

At the appointed hour I found myself awake, sorely tempted to remain for a few more minutes, but, nervous that I might oversleep, I pitched out of my bed roll. There is something rather horrible about rising at 1.30 a.m. when one is in the deepest trough of sleep, especially when the body is weary from the exertions of the previous day. I looked out of the tent-flap at the solitude of the landscape, bathed in the light of the glorious full moon. Already shadows were moving around me and Mackland arrived with a canvas bucket of water and I was soon shaving.

It was cold and I felt nervous. Sergeant Neil came across to advise me that my troop was almost ready. We breakfasted on bully beef and biscuits with water – no tea being allowed as fires might betray our position to the enemy. The horses having been fed and watered, saddling up began and we were soon ready to mount.

My squadron leader, Captain Jervoise Scott, called us up for orders. By now we knew that our offensive up the Euphrates had been timed to coincide with Allenby's push in Palestine. Thus the Turks and Germans would be engaged with equal pressure on two fronts, preventing them switching forces from one to the other. Our target was Khan Baghdadi on the bend of the river. The advance of the 11th Cavalry Brigade, the Guides leading, commenced at 3 a.m. and we set off in a north-north-easterly direction. At 5.30 a.m. with the dawn breaking, Cassels changed direction west, cutting into the desert, leaving the infantry to make their frontal assault on the enemy.

As the sun rose, it revealed an observation balloon rising slowly from General Brooking's headquarters. We were moving at a fast trot over boulder-strewn, trackless desert which was hard on the horses' legs. Soon we had reached a wide *wadi* which ran east and west to Baghdadi; this indicated that we were now immediately on the flank of the Turkish defenders.

Suddenly the enemy's field artillery opened fire and it seemed reasonable to suppose that the Turks had caught a glimpse of the Guides, who were protecting our right flank and were that much closer to the enemy. As a few desultory shells pitched harmlessly into the desert, we continued with pace unabated until suddenly 'W' Battery were ordered to halt and reply to the gunfire.

At 11.15 a.m. a message reached us from General Brooking to say that the Turks 50th Division appeared in no mood to retreat. The Turk is a stubborn fighter, especially in defence, and he seldom surrenders unless completely outfought. However, our task was to continue on into the desert, making a vast detour until we reached the next bend in the river near Alus, where we would sit astride the Aleppo road to cut off any retreat should the enemy decide to try to break out to the north.

About mid-day, the advance squadron of the Guides arrived at the Wadi Houran, very deep and wide, running across the desert from east to west, into the Euphrates, but dry at the moment. The sides were precipitous and as a report had been received that Turkish infantry were withdrawing down the *wadi* towards the Aleppo road, a reconnaissance had to be made for a crossing place.

At this point reconnaissance patrols were sent out to ascertain the position on the right and soon returned with the information that a battallion of Turkish infantry were astride the *wadi* a mile or so to the east, no doubt the force reported earlier. The Guides Cavalry, supported by 'W' Battery, were ordered to attack this force, while the remainder of the brigade crossed the *wadi* to gain the Aleppo Road.

It was now the turn of my own squadron to 'trail the shirt', in other words, to lead the advance. Jervoise, normally referred to as 'Snicker' Scott, gave the command and we trotted forward, one section way out in front to attract the fire of any enemy in the vicinity. We had hardly crossed the Wadi Houran when orders came in from Cassels that we should immediately change direction eastwards in order to gallop forward to get astride the road. Unfortunately, Cassels had miscalculated the distance and Scott, realizing that it was not in the immediate vicinity, steadied down the pace, until suddenly the leading section ran into the adjutant of the Guides, who appeared from the right. He informed them that the hill we were approaching was occupied by Turks. A few moments later and the leading troop, commanded by Lieutenant Tomkin, came under fire. We galloped to dead ground, dismounting ready for action. Snicker shouted to me to come over, his speech clipped and to the point. 'Porchey, take charge of the led horses and also the Hotchkiss gun troop. See that depression over there? Get 'em all under cover. Remain with them until we see which way this fight develops, but be ready in case we need the horses in a hurry. For God's sake, don't let them get shot up!'

By now, bullets were beginning to whine about our ears. The horses trembled with excitement and fear. Lowry Payne-Galway took charge of the rest of the squadron. In the confusion, it was difficult to know quite what was happening but, as our squadron fanned out and began to advance over the rising ground, the intensity of the fire increased. Carrying out my orders, I soon had the horses reasonably safe and secure, no easy task amid the developing din and rattle of the fighting. After ten minutes, I decided to leave them in the charge of the farrier sergeant-major and make my way forward to see how the fight was going.

I dodged from boulder to boulder until, after a few hundred yards, I reached the crest of the ridge. Here bullets were ricocheting while our men were firing all round me. Making a last spring, I topped the rise and hurled myself down behind a boulder on the forward slope. It was to find that I was in the midst of my own troop and, as I dropped to the sand, I heard one of my men mutter, 'Got you, you bastard!' I raised my head for an instant which coincided with another burst of fire and instinctively I flattened behind my cover. Not a second too soon, I was to find out half an hour later, for a bullet had drilled a neat hole through the top of my helmet. Three inches lower and I should not now be recounting this story.

Unaware of my narrow escape, I again raised myself on my elbows and this time felt very windy for, until this moment, I had seen no sign of the enemy. The cause of my concern was a good view of the Turkish defenders coming forward to attack us. We were separated by something like four hundred yards.

Suddenly the tempo of our shooting increased. For a minute or two it seemed that the Turks were escaping until, quite suddenly, there were no longer any of them standing on their feet. Seizing the initiative, we jumped up and began to pick our way forward amidst the groans of the wounded.

Before me lay the body of a dead Turkish officer, and around his neck was a pair of Zeiss binoculars. Without a moment's hesitation, I slipped the strap from over his head and looped it round my own neck. It was to be the only piece of loot that I would obtain from the Mesopotamian campaign, and to this very day I never visit a racecourse without them.

Our instructions were to hold the hill and safeguard any attempt by the enemy to break out into the desert. For our squadron 'A', the initial battle was over. Our sister squadron 'B' was well in front but, as yet, not within sight of the Aleppo road which was our prime objective. At 3.15 Cassels went forward to find that further advance was blocked by a fair-sized hill and he gave instructions that it should be captured. Having successfully crossed the intervening ground, they dismounted at the bottom of the hill and advanced in open order, charging over the top. They found it unoccupied and took up positions on the forward slope. It was very fortunate for them that the hill was undefended.

There was still no sign of a road and 'B' Squadron continued to occupy the hill, sending out a reconnaissance patrol to locate the road and cut the telegraph line if possible. It was nearly 4 p.m. and Cassels decided he must strike inwards towards the road and river and 'C' Squadron (Captain Breitmeyer) were ordered to wheel right. A mile or so further on, they encountered enemy fire and had to make for cover. Breitmeyer staged an attack but the Turks put up a strong defence and 'D' Squadron had to be sent to support them. Cassels was dissatisfied with the situation since, at the moment when he needed concentration, his units were widely dispersed. The essential was to get a foothold on the road and then concentrate on that foothold. 'B' Squadron were ordered to get to the road as soon as possible, whilst we moved to 'B's old position, enabling three squadrons of the regiment to be ready to back up 'B'.

'B' Squadron set off at a steady trot, the horses beginning to be footsore on the hard stony ground. Evans became more and more anxious as time went on and there was nothing to guide him, when suddenly through his glasses he saw two tiny specks – telegraph poles. About five o'clock, they were on a crest with the Aleppo road two or three hundred yards below them. To the north, the road disappeared behind a rocky crest and to the south, towards the enemy, it was open and exposed on a sloping plateau before dropping out of sight behind a rocky ridge half a mile away. This seemed a good natural position for defence and sections were posted to left, right and in the rear, the remainder of the force taking mutually supporting positions. There was not a rifle in reserve but the dispositions would present the greatest possible display of force to a tired enemy in retreat.

After some difficulty, contact was established with Cassels and shallow trenches were dug in the hard and stony ground, sufficient to give some cover to men kneeling in them. Cassels sent another squadron to reinforce 'B' and kept the rest of the force concentrated.

As light was fading, a column was seen a thousand yards away and when it had approached to three hundred yards, the squadron leader opened fire with devastating results. There was no resistance and cries of surrender arose above the din. When the dust settled, it was seen that the 'guns' were travelling kitchens and the 'cavalry' were transport with pack animals. The fifty or sixty prisoners taken were very co-operative and in spite of language difficulties, it was learned that the Turkish 50th Division were pulling out of their position at Khan Baghdadi and were in retreat along the Aleppo road 'in many, many thousands'.

The action had achieved complete success, but the squadron leader feared that the firing had given away his position to the enemy and that he could be over-run by their superior numbers. Fortunately, the firing had acted as a beacon to Breitmeyer, who was able to bring up 'C' Squadron immediately. It was decided that 'C' Squadron should close the gap between 'B' and the river and so hold off Turkish reinforcements that might be coming down from the west, while 'B' concentrated their strength on a narrower front.

By now, night had fallen and the troops, tired and cold, having been on the move since three o'clock in the morning, huddled in the shallow trenches eating the little that remained of their haversack rations and anything edible from the Turkish ration carts.

Two miles or so to the right, the bulk of the 11th Cavalry Brigade were concentrated. The Guides Cavalry were still at the Wadi Houran but the remaining units were ready to support 'B' and 'C' Squadrons on the Aleppo road, or to attack the Turks if they tried to escape to the open desert.

Cassels sent a summary of his positions to General Brooking at 9.30 p.m. The enemy were still resisting strongly the pressure of the 15th Indian Division, but Brooking, knowing the Turks were at a complete disadvantage, kept up the pressure and awaited his opportunity.

The Squadron Leader of 'B' Squadron had sat staring along the road, silvery under the full moon, for what seemed an eternity, when out of the shadow of the ridge half a mile away, a black blob appeared, spread a little and crept onwards along the road, getting larger as it came and eventually became a column of horsemen advancing at a walk, unsuspecting. Whispered orders and a quick hustle through the trenches, and at two hundred yards an inferno broke out from rifles and machine guns. The column crumbled, ragged groups fleeing for cover. The rout was complete and the enemy made no further effort to cross the plateau, having apparently concluded that their only escape would be by way of the open desert. Hence, some hours after the fighting on the plateau died down, 'A' and 'D' squadrons saw large numbers of the enemy approaching some two miles to the right. The Turks were again surprised at close range and after finding themselves attacked in flank, they gave up and the Turkish 50th Division ceased to be a fighting formation.

At 10.15 p.m. a message arrived from General Brooking that the enemy were in general retreat from Khan Baghdadi and Cassels was to block all escape routes, whilst preparations were made to carry out a rapid advance towards Ana, where the Turks were reported to have an advanced base. When, after an uneventful if difficult march, the 7th Hussars reached Ana in the early afternoon of 27 March, they found that the Turks had fled the previous day, leaving large dumps of stores and ammunition.

There is only one more story to tell of this, my baptism of fire. After we had collected all the prisoners and seized much stored ammunition that the Turks would have used in their attack on Baghdad, we came upon a huge open cave in the cliff face. Within it was a sight almost too horrific to describe.

For reasons which we were unable to ascertain, some two or three hundred Arabs had collected in this vast natural cavern, so starved and emaciated that they could not even be compared to the victims of Belsen. Possibly a third of them were already dead; the others were littered upon the ground, literally within hours or minutes of death. Their skin was translucent, to such a degree that the outline of every vital organ in their bodies could easily be seen. Even our hardened soldiers were so aghast that they immediately set about trying to help them. Taking in water and condensed milk, they endeavoured to feed those able to lift their heads. Their condition was such that upon accepting the nourishment they fell back dead. In some dreadful instances their stomachs actually burst. How or why they had reached this condition we knew not, but the nearby cluster of village huts contained no food. Presumably the occupying army had consumed all their stores so that they had received absolutely no nourishment for weeks. The term 'a living skeleton' was never more appropriate.

There was still one more shot to be fired. A day or two after this battle, in the middle of the night, one of our troopers had good reason to visit the latrines but, sleepily threading his way through the boulders, took the wrong path. As he wandered about, a sentry heard his movements.

Being dressed overall in khaki, the soldier could not be

seen. The sentry, now fully alert, waited for what he was certain must be an enemy intent upon infiltrating our lines.

The trooper, failing to find the latrines and unable to wait any longer, dropped his trousers and began to squat. The rays of the moon caught his untanned posterior and to the sentry there was a sudden flash of white. Drawing a bead, as if on snap shooting practice, he fired a rapid single shot, to be rewarded by a piercing scream and a very English oath.

The camp was roused to find that one cavalryman's buttocks had been neatly drilled by a bullet. Fortunately, no bones were broken and the wound was clean; but at least one trooper would have to forgo the saddle for a good six weeks.

7
The Death of Sausage

After a few days' rest at Dhibban, the regiment moved to a patch of desert some fifty miles from Baghdad on the bank of the Euphrates, called Sheik Habib. Here our task was to build a camp and remain throughout the stifling heat of summer, with temperatures again rising from one hundred and fifteen to one hundred and twenty degrees.

In September I received a summons to present myself at GHQ, Baghdad. Having had sand-fly fever, I was not feeling too fit, but the journey to the capital would make a change and I was curious as to the reason why I had been singled out. Next morning I reported to a Military Intelligence Colonel and he explained why I had been summoned. Because of my ability to speak French fluently I had been designated a Grade A interpreter. In recognition of this qualification I received a ten pound per annum bonus.

'Porchester, we have a highly confidential and rather unusual task for you to perform, but before going into any detail, I must warn you that you are under the Official Secrets Act and must disclose the details to no one.'

My curiosity aroused, I nodded, while for his part the Colonel endeavoured to judge my response.

'As you probably know, there's been a revolution in Russia

and the Bolsheviks are sweeping across the country. The White Russians are still our allies, but they are being desperately hard pressed and are short of food, ammunition and money.

'Now, one of the White Russian Divisions is under the command of a man called General Baratoff. He is one of Wrangel's men and His Majesty's Government, after very careful consideration, has decided to send him a consignment of gold. Your task will be to escort and convey this bullion some four hundred miles to a place called Enzeli, a little village on the shore of the Caspian Sea. Baratoff understands a little French, but his ADC speaks it fluently. This is the reason you have been chosen.'

The Colonel paused, and I tried hard to contain my excitement at the prospect of making my escape from the desperate monotony of our present existence.

The Colonel cleared his throat and continued:

'You will take two young officers with you, one of whom is skilled in cipher and will be in charge of the wireless unit, while the second will arrange your transport. Your own troop will act as guard and escort.

'But it's not just a question of delivering the gold, although this is your primary task. I shall want you to entertain General Baratoff and we shall provide you with the necessary funds.

'What we are anxious to learn from the General's own lips is just how much more fight is left in the White Russian Army. They've had a pretty hard time and the revolution is in the balance, with the scales tilted in favour of a Bolshevik victory. We, of course, support the Old Order, but our concern is not so much to become involved in the domestic strife but to ensure that our allies maintain their pressure on our common enemy. We must be in a position to judge for just how much longer this can be relied upon.

'I understand that you are reasonably good at map-reading but, take care, it's a long journey and you can afford no mistakes. The terrain is the usual featureless desert, and you'll be damned glad to see the sea at the end of it. You will guard that gold with your life. Enclosed in this envelope are your written instructions together with a formal receipt to which you will obtain General Baratoff's signature; make sure you get it. We estimate that the outward leg will take you two weeks. Now, let's have a look at these maps and I'll go over your route.'

I posed question after question until I felt that I was thoroughly briefed.

Three days later we set out, shrouded in secrecy. Sergeant Neil, a veteran of the Boer War, was a positive godsend, always alert and helpful. The journey was to prove uneventful as we crossed the limitless desert of Northern Persia. However, we could not force the pace, held back by the speed of the two horse-drawn wagons carrying the gold.

As we neared the Caspian the country began to change, with more fertile ground, clumps of palms and an increasing number of villages. At last the undulating ground began to dip to the shore of the inland sea and we reached the outskirts of Enzeli. Setting up camp just outside the town, we awaited the arrival of the Russians.

Using my funds of local money, I visited the market and purchased caviar, vodka, a few bottles of Caucasian wine and other supplies. In addition, we obtained the luxury of fresh fruit, some chickens and a quantity of good vegetables. For the men, and indeed myself, this was the food of the gods.

When on the appointed day the Russians failed to appear, I decided to communicate with Baghdad. We encoded a message to the effect that we had safely reached our destination but that there was no sign of our contacts. The signal was not acknowledged and it was with a sense of relief that, in the late afternoon of the second day, a messenger ran into my tent to announce their arrival.

Baratoff was a small man with a somewhat square head and he was accompanied by his ADC. They had ridden into camp alone. The General wore the astrakhan hat of the Cossacks, a greatcoat and, strapped round his waist, two outsized Mauser automatics. Although glad to see me, he seemed generally depressed. He was, however, obviously relieved that we had brought the gold which had been promised. His ADC was a better educated man who had been to the Officers' School at St Petersburg. He was older than I, possibly twenty-eight, good-looking and spoke fluent French.

In the early evening we sat down to dinner. Before doing so, I had tried to persuade the General to divest himself of his weapons; but he remained obdurate and explained that he would not be parted from them. During the meal I learnt that his troops had little or nothing to eat, their uniforms were in rags and could not be replaced and that his soldiers had received no pay for the last eighteen months. 'Will they fight?' I asked, to which he replied that nothing was certain any longer. If we had brought paper roubles there would have been little chance at all but as he would be returning with gold, he believed that the prospects were brighter.

His ADC explained, for Baratoff understood French but could not speak it, that a company of Cossacks would arrive in the morning with suitable transport. He also suggested that as the two of them had travelled a long way, they would be glad of an early night's rest. While pleasant, the evening could not be described as a sparkling success, for Baratoff seemed generally demoralized and in low spirits.

The following morning, shortly after dawn, the Cossacks appeared, an ill-assorted, unkempt lot, their discipline at low ebb. The boxes of bullion were loaded on their wagons, the receipt was signed and, after shaking hands, the Russians left. The countryside being so inhospitable, we were happy to saddle up the horses and commence the long ride back to Baghdad.

I cannot say that I thought much had been accomplished and history would seem to indicate that perhaps, this time, I was right.

On return to the regiment, we found the general belief was that the war would soon be ended but the war against Turkey was being reviewed and on 4 October 1918, a warning order was received by 11th Cavalry Brigade, which still included the 7th Hussars. This action was to mark the end of our regiment's two hundred years' fighting in the saddle, although we didn't realize this at the time.

As it happened, during the summer months I had been detailed to attend a cipher course and now found myself separated from my unit in that I was attached to General Cassels as his cipher officer. Among my wireless unit, a number of whom were Australians, was Sergeant Victor MacLaughlan, who was to become a film star and achieve worldwide fame in *Four Feathers*.

The following day, 5 October, the regiment received their orders to move. Their strength consisted of twenty officers, four hundred and sixty-six other ranks and five hundred and fifty horses. For my part, I was at Brigade HQ, never more than a few yards from Cassels.

Also attached to his staff was Colonel Leetchman who was the British political officer for the area, speaking fluent Arabic and Turkish. He was a remarkable man and knew the country well. As we advanced, the Colonel picked up an Arab guide to help him.

By 18 October, the 11th Cavalry Brigade had arrived at Al Agik on the right bank of the Tigris, some eighty miles upstream of Baghdad, having marched one hundred and twenty miles. On 20 October our brigade received orders from Cassels to continue to Tekrit.

At 3.0 a.m. on 23 October, the 7th Hussars left Tekrit and marched off in the darkness as the main regiment of the Brigade, making for the Ain Nukailah Pass. It was 6 p.m. on the following day before 'C' Squadron, last squadron of all, having travelled through the Pass, rejoined the regiment at Ain Khalid, a point chosen because of the springs of water there. The water, supposed to be 'sweet' turned out to be impregnated with Epsom Salts, with dire results for both men and horses.

Thirty-five miles to the north lay the Lesser Zab over

which a bridgehead was to be established and we began crossing the desert in heat such as none of us had experienced before. Having been unable to refill water bottles, both men and horses had to remain without any moisture at all. Rations at breakfast had been minimal – biscuits and jam. As the day wore on our lips became cracked and bleeding, but the redoubtable Leetchman at no time even put a topee on his head. Thin and sinewy, he seemed impervious to these inhuman conditions.

Now it was the turn of my own regiment to lead the Brigade and it became necessary to decide at what point the Zab should be forded. The Arab guide persisted in indicating one precise position and it was obvious that Leetchman did not entirely trust him.

Gradually we drew nearer and when two or three miles away, the General called me over. 'Porchey, these horses are going mad with thirst; I've had experience of this sort of thing before. It's your regiment up front; I want you to canter ahead and take this message to William Gibbs. Tell him to warn the men that when the horses smell the water they may well get out of hand. By the time you reach them they won't be far short of the river. Tell Gibbs that whatever happens, he must get over and secure himself on the opposite bank.' Cassels was quite calm in spite of the fact that he was also suffering badly from the heat. I remember him smoking cigarettes incessantly.

It took me twenty minutes to reach my regiment and report to Colonel Gibbs but I had hardly given him Cassels's warning when, all of a sudden, the leading horses took off, completely out of control as predicted. As they began to charge forward, Sausage leapt to follow the rest. We were on the upper end of an undulating slope, stretching some four hundred yards to the water's edge.

Maddened with thirst, riders and beasts hurled themselves into the river and, amidst a *mêlée* of horses and men, I found myself doing likewise. With topees knocked off and troopers being pitched into the water, the confusion was utterly indescribable. The distance between the sandstone banks was approximately forty yards.

Suddenly, the shallow ravine began to erupt with the shattering explosion of rifles, machine-guns, and even the odd piece of artillery. Cupping the water in my hand, slaking my thirst, throwing it over my face, I and the rest of the regiment totally ignored the enemy until suddenly the water began to be stained a violent crimson. Horses and men alike were being caught in a lacerating cross fire. It was our turn to be engulfed in an ambush.

With a supreme effort to recover discipline, the officers bellowed to their men, the NCOs responded and we gradually extricated ourselves from the inglorious mess. The scene was a shambles but gradually the men forced their horses out of the water.

I galloped back to Brigade HQ to find that the column was halted. 'Ambush, sir,' I told Cassels. Standing beside him was Leetchman. Breathlessly I reported the situation.

'How many have we lost?'

'Probably not more than ten, sir. Maybe a dozen or so horses.'

'Damn bad show,' Bob Cassels retorted, 'bloody sods these Arab guides.'

On the strength of my report, Leetchman took the law into his own hands and shot the guide.

Cassels, who had taken a minute or two to sum up the situation, turned to me again.

'Look here, Porchey, you and your horse have had a drink. You can get cracking again. You should find 'W' Battery not much more than a mile to the rear. Go down there as fast as you can and get hold of Maclewain. Tell him to come up at full gallop and lead him to the best firing position. *You've* been there; you know better than I. Tell him all you can; tell him to unlimber the guns and start shelling as fast as he can.'

'Very good, General,' I said and galloped off.

Despite being shelled and machine-gunned *en route*, I

arrived unscathed and Andrew Maclewain, a friend of long standing, demanded what the hell was going on.

'There's been an ambush at the ford on the Zab. The Turks are firing from high ground on the opposite side of the river. The General wants you to take the battery up forward as fast as possible, unlimber and start shooting.'

'Very good.' Turning in his saddle, he shouted some orders pointing in the general direction. 'Come on, Porchey, you'd better show us where they are.'

In the meantime, Cassels had called up the one spotter biplane attached to us which, fortunately, had been standing by at General Brooking's headquarters.

The little plane was already circling high above the Turkish positions when we reached our vantage point, aware that the enemy were still firing. Suddenly we heard the plane's engine cough, splutter, then die away. A lucky rifle shot had hit the fuel tank.

In a desperate endeavour to find some boulder-free ground, the pilot banked steeply to make a crash landing on our side of the river which, by a miracle, he managed to achieve. However, he was in plain view of the Turks who immediately opened up with rifle and machine-gun fire. The range was about half a mile and there appeared to be no hope for the pilot who scrambled out of the cockpit and ran for about thirty yards before throwing himself on to the ground.

My attention was attracted by a movement some two or three hundred yards ahead. To my astonishment, I saw my old friend Brit trotting out from behind the cover into which he had manœuvred his squadron. Sitting erect in his saddle, he broke into a steady canter, apparently impervious to the rapidly increasing shell fire.

All eyes watched in silent consternation as Brit closed the distance between himself and the bi-plane. Never once did he change his pace. After what seemed like an age, although in effect it was only a few minutes, he reached his destination, unscathed. The pilot jumped up from behind a boulder, leapt on behind his rescuer and both returned unhurt. Brit was awarded an MC for his gallantry.

Almost before I knew it, the guns of 'W' Battery RHA were coming up behind us, directed by Maclewain into a reasonably secure position where they were quickly unlimbered and opened fire on the Turks. Wheeling my horse, I returned to headquarters.

'Well done,' said Cassels. 'Now I want you to go to your Colonel and tell him the following: he must immediately resume crossing the river, making every effort to do so in good order under cover of the bombardment that Mack is giving him. Depending upon the amount of light left available, he should follow up the Turks who, I imagine, will be retreating and, if the opportunity arises, they are to draw swords and charge. D'you get me?'

'God,' I thought, 'this is a bit much. Exhausted horses, tired men, a rotten position to attack. But this is no business of mine. Draw swords and charge.'

'Very good, sir,' I said, to which the General replied, 'Go on then, get cracking. No time to lose!'

For the third time I climbed into the saddle, so hot that if you touched it with your bare hand you were in danger of receiving blisters, and rode off to find William Gibbs again. By this time, Maclewain's shells were bursting across the ridge, but whether the enemy was still in position it was indeed difficult to tell. I found the Colonel, to whom I delivered the message. He appeared unruffled although he raised his eyebrows.

'Did he, by Jove!' was his laconic reply at the thought of our charging tactics. 'Now look here, Porchey, we'll need you for this attack. Get forward as fast as you can and take over your troop.'

This was hardly the news I was expecting. However, I made my way to my troop who seemed well pleased to see me.

'You've been having a cushy time, sir,' they chorused. 'Are you back for good?'

'I don't know about cushy time,' I exploded, 'and the answer is "no". I'm just visiting for the evening's entertainment. I hope your swords are sharp; we're about to cross the river and put in a charge!'

'Charge?' they chorused. 'What are you talking about?'

'You fellows don't know what they've got in store for you.'

'The General's mad,' they replied. 'Anyway, who are we going to charge and where?'

'The Turks,' I responded, 'on the other side of the river.'

'If you can find them, sir. They aren't going to stay up there with old Mack pounding them.'

'I hope not for all our sakes. Anyway, we'll have to wait and see.'

Fortunately for us the Colonel had just previously sent an officers' patrol a mile down river where they had found another deep though passable ford. Gibbs decided to outflank the enemy position and cross lower down which he achieved with only slight opposition that had the effect of hastening the crossing. Having accomplished this with 'B' Squadron leading, we moved forward towards a ridge on the opposite bank. Here 'B' Squadron were smartly engaged by the Turks. As darkness descended, the enemy melted away.

During the night, a body of Turks came marching down the track across which the advanced squadrons were picketed. They met a withering fire and prisoners taken the following morning told them that some eight hundred Turks had been involved in the initial skirmish at the river. We had been lucky.

Cassels was eager to press on and as wireless messages began to stream in from the headquarters of the commander-in-chief, I was expected to work through the night to decode them. By morning, I was too exhausted to even think of sitting in a saddle and Cassels agreed that I should be given a space in a wagon in order to get some sleep.

The advance continued. However, one of the messages I decoded in the night informed the Brigadier that the troops in the south were meeting very determined resistance and that the enemy showed no sign of breaking. It was now imperative for Cassels to advance to a good defensive feature, in order to be ready for whatever might befall.

It was three days later that the Brigadier, standing on top of a small hill, could see far away to the north-west a low ridge which, from his primitive sketch map, seemed to indicate the high ground at Huwaish which stood on the right bank of the Tigris beyond the Wadi Muabbah. 'If I could get that position, I could hold the whole Turkish Army,' I heard Cassels mutter. The Tigris was wide at this point and the current strong. The Brigadier plunged into the water, leaving part of 'W' Battery to cover the crossing and ordering me to remain, because it was impossible to get the wireless vehicle across the uneven, boulder-strewn bottom.

By 7.30 that night most of the brigade were in position and I began encoding our first outgoing message. In this, Cassels was reporting his latest move in order that his supporting transport columns could reach him with ammunition, food and fodder. Our supplies were running low.

Late in the night I received a wireless message that was marked with a 7.30 p.m. transmission time. It informed us of three important developments: the first that a pontoon bridge building operation was running into difficulties and our transport column could not be expected to arrive on time; the second that the 18th Indian Division which was supposed to be coming up to join him was still on the other side of the Lesser Zab; lastly that the 7th Cavalry Brigade had been withdrawn to move into mobile reserve. By the time I had finished the decoding it was well into the morning. The General's reaction was muted. He immediately sent a reply requesting to be kept informed, with an urgent plea for eighteen-pounder ammunition as 'W' Battery were beginning to run short.

By 8 a.m. on 27 October, Cassels had most of his troops in position at Huwaish but a dawn patrol, sent out to probe to the south, made contact with a fair-sized body of the enemy, estimated at five hundred riflemen, at least three field-artillery guns and several machine-gun sections.

The General instructed the squadron to remain in contact and, if necessary, to attack the Turks by way of harassment, in order not to betray his own comparative weakness. Yet another message warned of a possible advance by the enemy from Mosul in the north. Cassels immediately sent out an officers' patrol to the northwards to verify the situation.

Having progressed some ten or eleven miles without seeing any sign of the enemy, the patrol came to a small hill. Trotting to the top of it, the officer in command looked down over a wide expanse of plain. On it, and advancing in their direction, was a long column of infantry, whose strength he estimated at not less than four hundred men. It appeared that now we were very much the ham in the sandwich and something would have to be done.

Working on the old military axiom that the best form of defence is to attack, and such a policy fitting the character of the General, Cassels immediately sent the 23rd Cavalry to attack the Turks advancing from the south. 'Put the fear of God into them,' was his instruction, 'but avoid too many casualties. Your task is simply a delaying action.' But they were biting off much more than they could chew for after an initial skirmish it was estimated that the enemy force comprised at least one thousand riflemen, supported by four pieces of field artillery and many machine-guns.

Looking to the north, Cassels decided that another delaying action was required. He contacted Colonel Gibbs who, in turn, allocated the task to 'C' Squadron, commanded by Alan Breitmeyer. This operation Brit executed brilliantly by galloping from position to position, dismounting, appearing over a crest or ridge, opening fire upon the enemy and then melting away again.

I was still marooned on the other side of the river with the wireless vehicles, remote and alone, save for my very small staff. At 3 p.m. we received a radio message to confirm that a column of Turks were indeed moving south from

Mosul. It was going to be a race against time. Cassels was now fighting for our lives. The fire from the enemy was beginning to increase in tempo, both to the north and the south. It was not long before I could actually see the infantry through my field glasses, coming towards us from Mosul.

Although it would be a pitiful effort, I decided to take ten men a short distance up to the north, with Huwaish on my right on the other bank of the river, and open up intermittent fire in support of Breitmeyer. I cannot imagine it had any effect, but at least the Turks would think that there were forces in opposition on the far side of the river. After half an hour's desultory action, I returned to the wireless vehicle. Still more calls were coming in, one of which was to inform us that our old Colonel, now Brigadier-General Norton, was coming to our support. This news was very welcome.

With a considerable collection of messages, I realized that the time had come when I must cross the river and deliver them personally to the General. Telling Sergeant Victor McLaughlan to remain in his position and calling Mackland to join me, I saddled up Sausage, placed the messages in a waterproof container and moved down to the riverbank. I was never a good swimmer and the prospects of the crossing were daunting. Several men had been swept away and, after the passage of so many cavalry, the bottom was now disturbed and uncertain. Plunging in, we were soon in deep water and, slipping from my saddle, I left the main exertion to Sausage. The instinct for survival is as strong in a horse as it is in his rider. Gradually he fought his way across the swift-flowing current, found a footing and gamely lurched up the far side. So far, no-one had spotted us. Mackland had been covering my crossing and I was now out in the open. I knew it would only be seconds before I was seen.

Leaping into the saddle, I sent Sausage on his way with a kick, the sound of distant rifles and machine-guns heightening my anticipation and fear. We had just reached the halfway mark when the Turkish machine-gunners got our range. Bullets began whining around my ears, kicking up spurts of sand or ricocheting from the odd boulders in our path. We were now galloping flat out.

Suddenly Sausage gave a ghastly lurch and I was hurled from the saddle. With the wind knocked out of me, I saw my charger kicking in his death throes. As bullets still spattered around the sand, I got behind poor Sausage and lay quite still. For a few more seconds the machine-gunners persisted, until obviously they thought we must both be dead. Moving carefully to my saddle-bag, I extracted one precious tin of Three Castles cigarettes and my message container. Fortunately they had not been hit.

Squirming round, I looked back to see if there was any sign of Mackland. By the time he had crossed the river my horse had already been shot and he realized that it would be fatal to follow. He thus waited within the protective banks of the river, deciding that he might be able to retrieve the saddle and equipment under cover of night. Slipping the tin of cigarettes into a pocket, I prepared to make my dash. It occurred to me at first that I might try crawling, but, as I moved away from the horse, the heat of the sand was so unbearable and my progress so slow that I decided to throw caution to the winds. Scrambling to my feet, I broke into a run and had made approximately just over half the distance when a Turkish machine-gun once again began to chatter.

I accelerated madly. With the bullets singing round my ears and kicking up the sand, I tried to dodge and weave, but with lungs now bursting and about one hundred and fifty yards to go, I abandoned the tactic. I was now sprinting with every ounce of energy called up from my reserves, the blood pounding in my temples. Suddenly I heard cheers of encouragement and ribald laughter as, with the last kick I had in me, I crashed over the mounds of our shallow positions.

I felt weak and faint and lay where I had fallen, gasping at the hot desert air in a vain effort to recharge my lungs. It was some minutes before I realized that I was safe.

'Well done, Porchey,' a friend called, 'you'll be in the Olympics with good old Burleigh if we live through this one.'

Having collected myself, I made my way to Cassels and gave my messages to him. He had already heard of my exploits and said, 'Well done, well done; glad you were able to join us. I say, I suppose you don't happen to have any cigarettes?'

'Well, as a matter of fact, General, I did manage to bring a few.'

'Hand 'em over, dear boy,' he said, 'we're in one hell of a jam and if I can't get us out of this, you won't have any need of them.'

I did not care much for his remarks and passed them over like lightning. Immediately he had lit a cigarette, he opened up the canister and took out the messages. Puffing vigorously, he studied them.

'Hm,' he said, 'looks as if Charles Norton may get here before long. That'll be useful. My God, we need him. Look, Porchey, you see that Observation Post over there?'

'N-no, General, I'm afraid I can't see where you mean.'

'Over there, dear boy,' he said pointing, 'it's the gunners' OP. In it you should find Maclewain or one of his officers. I instructed them to go very carefully with the ammunition. Tell them not to worry quite so much and if they see any good opportunities not to miss 'em. When you've done that, come back and I'll let you know what the next job is.'

'This man's a menace,' I thought. 'Not a moment's respite.' But out I went to do as instructed and soon found Mack.

'You've had some fun,' he laughed.

'I don't know about fun,' I replied, 'it was a damn close thing and now the Old Man is pressing me back into work.'

'Well, why not stay up here? You can watch all that's going on.'

I told him that it looked just possible that reinforcements might soon be reaching us.

'Bloody-well time, I reckon,' was his pointed reply. 'God, we've lost some men. Geoffrey Hallowes has gone and so many other good chaps.'

The following day, I had to replace Sausage. Later that night Mackland had been able to join me, having retrieved my saddle.

I went in search of the farrier-major, whose name was Pickard, and found him with the led horses. He offered me the pick of the bunch and I chose a Waler. I began to walk back to Brigade HQ when, with a crump, a shell landed just behind me which killed poor Pickard.

For five more days we fought at Huwaish with dwindling food and next to no ammunition until Saunders reached us with the 53rd Infantry Brigade. On 30 October, the 7th Hussars – now down to three squadrons only – once more found themselves saddling up in the dark. Happily, at daylight, white flags were waving in the desert: the commander of the Turkish forces on the Tigris had finally surrendered.

When the news came through, I was with General Cassels. I was stunned by the losses we had suffered. When you have lived, worked and fought together as a regiment for year after year, you become the greatest of friends. Turning to the General I said, 'What a tragedy, when we're so near the end of the war, to think of so many of my pals being killed.'

For the first time since I had been with him, Cassels rounded on me. 'Listen,' he said, 'you cannot make omelettes without breaking eggs. We've done a damned good job and a very useful one. Remember this. How much better to be able to say to your grandchildren that you did your share, rather than that you sat on your arse and did nothing. At least you will have that satisfaction.'

Despondently, I rode across to rejoin my squadron.

Later, when the Colonel and I, accompanied by his trumpeter and my orderly, were engaged in collecting the identity discs and marking the position of the bodies awaiting burial,

I came upon the body of my dear friend, Geoffrey Hallowes, which was being desecrated by an Arab who was cutting off his boots. I was so incensed that I pulled out my revolver and shot him dead.

8
Green Fields

Cassels was informed by radio that the Turkish commander on the Tigris had surrendered his forces. 'Exploit your victory to the utmost' was the message he received from the C-in-C. This could only spell one thing to our General. Having read the handwritten message taken down by the wireless operator, he turned with a grin of triumph: 'Right – it's flat out for Mosul.'

I stood there, speechless. With my regiment reduced by fifty per cent and all other units equally affected, I failed to see how we could do it. Mosul was fifty miles away. There was no such doubt in Cassels's mind; squadrons were amalgamated. On the morning of 31 October, the regiment once again saddled up in the dark and the advance on Mosul began. That night we bivouacked twelve miles south of the city, our innermost fears aroused in the knowledge that tomorrow, on the eve of victory, we would risk our lives again. We could see no point in taking Mosul: Cassels thought otherwise.

Having encoded a last message, I staggered to my tent and collapsed into an uneasy slumber. Hardly had I fallen asleep when I felt my shoulders being shaken.

'For Heaven's sake, leave me alone.'

'Sir,' the voice kept insisting, 'a long message has just come in.'

'Bloody hell! What on earth is it now? Okay, I'm coming.'

Fumbling for my torch, I went to the wireless tent, took out the code books and began deciphering. As my pencil moved across the message pad, I felt a sudden thrill.

> To Brigadier-General Cassels. Have to inform you enemy has sued for general armistice. His Majesty's Government has concurred. All troops to stand fast at their appointed positions 0800 this day. Terms of armistice for delivery to Commander of Turkish Sixth Army General Ali Ihsan Pasha in Mosul will be flown to you at approximately 0700 hours. You will take the terms of armistice in person accompanied by Brigadier-General Norton also Porchester acting as your interpreter. Understand he will be able to translate the said terms into colloquial French in order Turkish Commander-in-Chief left in no doubt as to our conditions. Acknowledge.

The silence in the tent was suddenly pierced by the loudest 'view hallo' probably ever recorded. It had happened at last, victory – peace – no more fighting. God, how wonderful!

I looked at my watch; it was only 3 a.m. Should I wake Cassels? 'Might not be too popular,' I thought, 'besides, what can he do at this ungodly hour. No, better to go to bed and get some sleep.' At 6 a.m. Mackland opened the tent to awaken me and I rose in the highest of spirits. 'Still plenty of time,' I thought, 'must look smart to convey this news to Cassels. I'll wash, shave and dress carefully.'

'It's all over,' I confided to my servant, 'but don't say a word until I've told the General.' 7 a.m. would be about the right time, I estimated; one whole hour before our instructions came into effect. Stepping out of my tent, I almost bumped into Colonel Thompson. He took one look at me and said, 'You're looking very pleased with yourself, Porchey.'

'So will you be, Colonel, when I tell you that the war is over.'

I brushed past him, as a look of amazement spread over his face. Fifty yards further on I came to the General's tent. He was standing outside and, giving him my smartest-ever salute, I said with a beaming smile, 'Good morning, General – glorious day. I have some very, very good news for you, Sir.'

'What's that?' he said, his eyes sparkling, and the thought rushed through my head that he might have been expecting to learn that he had been promoted to major-general.

'General,' I said, 'I am happy to be the first to inform you of the wonderful news that an Armistice has been signed. The war is over and we are not to move our positions from 0800 this morning.'

He stood rooted to the spot as if stupefied. Instead of a look of joy, his face took on an all-too-familiar thunderous expression. I could hardly believe my ears when I heard his words. What he said in measured tones, brooking no comment, was, 'I know nothing of this; I know *nothing* about this *whatsoever*. I've forgotten what you said. I haven't even heard it. Do you understand? I am going on to Mosul and nothing on earth will stop me!'

I was transfixed with horror and as he carefully watched my reaction, a thought suddenly occurred to him. He almost spat out the next sentence.

'I hope to God you haven't told anyone else?'

In a trice I saw my chance.

'Oh yes, General, as a matter of fact I have,' I said triumphantly. 'Indeed, I've told quite a number of people ...'

'You stupid little bugger. What the hell did you do that for? You should have kept your bloody mouth shut!'

'I'm so sorry, General ...'

'Christ,' he said, 'who have you told?'

'Well, sir, I ran into Colonel Thompson on my way over, only a few minutes ago, and before that I had told several others ...'

'Damn and blast you!' he raved and it was some minutes before his fury died down and he realized that I had thwarted, however innocently, his triumphal entry into Mosul.

In fact, he was not to be denied this pleasure. Some hours later, Cassels, Charles Norton, my own Colonel, William Gibbs, and I drove the last few miles to Mosul. When we arrived, we found a very smart guard of honour drawn up, with the Turkish staff officers and their General standing stiffly to attention. We approached them, returned their salutes, and I stepped forward and addressed Ihsan Pasha in French.

First, I introduced Cassels and Norton and explained that I was acting as interpreter and would be pleased to translate the terms of the Armistice from His Majesty's Government. Dressed in their very best uniforms, the Turks bowed and the General indicated that we should enter his headquarters. We sat round a large trestle table and Cassels told me to proceed. Glancing at my notes, and doing my best to translate the technical terms, I began to read the Instrument of Surrender, clause by clause. After about a quarter of an hour, I reached that part of the conditions which referred to the General and his senior officers. It said that after thirty-six hours of implementing the surrender of his forces, he was to enter a prisoner of war camp. I had just finished reading this clause when he suddenly raised his hand to interrupt me.

'*Un petit moment* ...' Speaking in French and somewhat ignoring Cassels and Norton, he said softly, 'Er, Lieutenant, please take note. I have the most lovely – she really is – the most lovely mistress any man could want. She is a beautiful girl, a Caucasian with soft white skin. Would you ask, as I shall not be allowed to take her into prison, whether General Norton would be so kind as to take her over and look after her appropriately.'

Trying desperately hard to keep my face straight, I began to translate into English. Interestingly, Ihsan had directed his words to Norton who was extremely handsome, tall and erect, whereas Cassels looked a much less attractive man. Norton's eyes twinkled and he swallowed several times. 'Porchey, you know Mary very well. You'd better explain to our friend that I don't think such a move would be considered very popular with my wife.'

Leaning back in my chair, I did my best to deliver a suitable reply, whereupon the General reluctantly looked at Cassels, but before he could open his mouth the Brigadier snapped, 'You don't know my wife, Porchey, but you can tell him from me, definitely *not*!'

I explained that the gentlemen regretted they were unable to accede to his request. He looked somewhat crestfallen and turning to me said, 'I am not going to let any junior officer have a jewel such as she.'

But then, after a pause, one last possibility occurred to him. 'You speak very good French; are you by any chance an English aristocrat?'

'Well, as a matter of fact, my father is Lord Carnarvon. I think he is quite well known in Turkey.'

Immediately, his eyes lit up.

'Then I give her to you,' he said with a magnanimous gesture.

I could not help laughing and replied, 'I'm awfully sorry, but I'm afraid it would not be allowed. But I'd love to have had her.'

At this remark, everyone burst into laughter. It had just subsided when the Turkish General went rigid and lifted his finger for silence. Wondering what on earth was afoot, we watched him quietly push back his chair, get to his feet and creep to the door. With a sudden movement, he turned the handle and hurled it open. Outside was one of his sentries, ear to the keyhole and caught in the act.

Without a perceptible pause, the General lashed forward with his boot and gave the man a kick in his backside, the like of which I have never seen before or since. The impact was such that the sentry took off through the air, complete with rifle and bayonet, and tumbled down eight or nine steps, fortunately managing to avoid impaling himself on his bayonet in the process. Ali Ihsan Pasha returned to the table and, as he sat down, said cheerfully, 'That will teach him to listen.'

The business finally completed, with signatures all round, we were invited to lunch. It was obvious that the Turks had really set out to please us. It was the first civilized meal I had had for ages. The first course consisted of a delicious pilau of chicken with beautifully prepared rice, courgettes, lettuce salad and fresh bread, something we had not tasted for months. For dessert we were given strawberries and cream. This was followed by Turkish coffee and Raffia. The sight of my friends applying themselves to second helpings of every dish the erstwhile enemy put before them warmed the cockles of my heart.

So ended the Mesopotamian Campaign in which Britain and the soldiers of her empire had conquered a vast area which extended from Basra in the south to Mosul in the north; from the Arabian desert to the Kurdish mountains and across the Caspian Sea. The cost to Britain and the empire had been ninety-seven thousand casualties. In my own regiment alone we had lost two hundred and twenty-four men killed, wounded, sick or missing, a wastage of over forty per cent.

In the regimental diary of the 7th Queen's Own Hussars, the following is noted: '*5 November 1918.* Mosul. Brigade in bivouac. Great shortage of forage and rations for horses and men respectively. *7 November 1918.* Mosul. On the night of 7/8 November the rain fell.' That evening I celebrated my twentieth birthday. Surely I was lucky to be alive.

The regiment rode back to Baghdad on half rations and I shared a small pup tent with Alan Breitmeyer. We both got dysentery.

A day or two after the Armistice, Alan told me that he had been given a Military Cross and that he had been told to award me the OBE. I was terrified of accepting it because, at that time, it was known as the 'Order of the Bad Egg'.

'In that case,' he said, 'if you don't want it, I shall suggest somebody else.'

You can imagine my feelings the following spring when, as acting adjutant at York, I received a letter from the War Office instructing me to inform the officer to whom it had been designated that he was to go to Buckingham Palace to be invested with a Military Cross as the deeds for which he had been recommended for the OBE were deserving of an MC.

On 24 March 1919, the 7th Queen's Own Hussars, reduced to twelve officers and ninety-six other ranks, left Baghdad by rail for Kut-el-Amara and thence by river steamer to Basra. The remainder of the journey home seemed interminable, Basra to Suez, then rail to Port Said where we spent eight days in an extremely dirty rest camp.

On the fourth night, I hung up my jacket as usual on the tent pole with four new ten pound notes in the left hand breast pocket and when I put it on in the morning, my forty pounds had disappeared and so had a lovely cigarette case which I valued highly. Regrettably, the cursed thief was never caught.

We had hoped to sail for England but instead were eventually deposited in a wretched, badly administered transit camp at Taranto in the heel of Italy. For the first time in several years we were setting foot on the continent of Europe and the reactions of officers and men to seeing a patch of green grass, after what seemed like aeons of time in the desert, must have provoked much mirth in the casual observer. We were so overjoyed and excited to see the greensward that when we could reach it, we rolled on it, such was our ecstasy.

In the worst collection of railway rolling stock imaginable, we jolted and rattled up through Italy and over the Alps into France. We duly reached Le Havre where we went through a delousing centre prior to embarking on a paddle steamer, in very rough weather, for the last few miles to Southampton.

During my absence abroad I had learned, from one of the

very few letters received, that Alfred de Rothschild had died and had bequeathed to my mother his beautiful house in Seymour Place, together with its priceless contents. Deciding upon a surprise return, I ventured to our new London home. The door was opened by Roberts.

'Good Heavens, m'Lord! How good to see you. What a surprise.'

The long expectation of reunion with my parents had blurred the memory of our past relationship. I had left as a boy; I returned as a man.

'Is her Ladyship in?'

'She is, m'Lord ... but she does have a guest, Colonel Arthur Bryant.'

Feeling somewhat peeved, I enquired, 'Shall I surprise them?'

'Well, m'Lord, perhaps you should first knock at the door, if I may suggest. Shall I take you up in the lift?'

Roberts opened the gates; I stepped inside and he pushed the button. I could feel my heart thumping with excitement as we came to a halt and Roberts pointed to a door. Smoothing down my hair, I knocked.

'Come in,' I heard my mother say.

As I pushed open the door it was to see my mother sitting on a stool in front of a mirror attending to her nails, while opposite, on a high-backed chair, sat the Colonel. He was a nice-looking man, of military bearing. As I stepped into the room, I noticed the look of surprise that swept across Almina's face.

'Oh darling, *what* a surprise!' For a moment she paused. 'My darling boy, where on earth have you come from?'

Slowly she stood up, not, as I was soon to realize, as a fond mother, but still as the matron in charge of her hospital.

'Good heavens, *where* have you come from in that dreadfully dirty uniform ...?' Then quickly, 'Have you been deloused?'

For a second I stood there, her remarks having the effect as of a bucket of ice-cold water thrown in my face.

'Deloused?' I found myself stammering. 'My darling mother, I have never seen a louse, let alone had one on my person. I can assure you we have been through all the quarantine formalities.'

'Are you quite sure?' she enquired. 'I mean, has your uniform been fumigated?'

'Yes, darling, it was fumigated at Le Havre.'

'Good. Now, tell us where you have been and what you have been doing all this time.'

9
Pleasures of Peace

For five weeks the regiment formed a cadre at Catterick Camp and then moved to the Cavalry Barracks in York. Our new CO was Lieutenant-Colonel Charles Rankin and he set about the not inconsiderable task of re-forming the regiment and bringing it up to strength. This required the recruitment of almost four hundred men and I was appointed acting adjutant.

We had only been home a month or two when my soldier servant, Mackland, died. I felt a real sense of personal loss as he had looked after me so well for so long.

We were extremely busy reorganizing but I had time to purchase a couple of hunters, hoping to hunt with the Bramham and the York and Ainsty. So far as the social scene was concerned no 'hunting' was necessary because, due to the ghastly loss of life in France, eligible bachelors were pursued by both mothers and daughters alike. For a free-booting subaltern, life was not without its attractions, but a subaltern bearing a title became a legitimate target for any number of adventures.

As spring arrived, the world began to look less grey and I met a girl of about my own age whose name was Flavia. Her mother was Lady Angela and I saw quite a lot of her and her mother. Flavia, however, was of the English tomboy type, slightly boisterous; so I never made a pass at her. We went to parties together, occasionally dined, but no more than that.

One day at York, the telephone rang. It was a call from her mother.

'Is that Lord Porchester?'

'It is,' I replied.

'Ah, Porchey, now look here; what I want to know is when are you going to announce your engagement to Flavia?'

I could hardly believe my ears.

'My dear Lady, what on earth are you talking about? Of course I am not about to announce our engagement. The thought of marrying has never entered my head. Anyway, why should I?'

'Why should you? Why should you indeed? What next are you going to say – really! A cavalry officer and a gentleman speaking like that about a girl he has betrayed!'

For a moment I was too surprised to become angry, the accusation being so fantastic.

'What on earth do you mean? I have never touched Flavia. I simply don't know what you are talking about.'

'Well, that's not what I understand.'

'Look here, all I can tell you is that every word I have said is true. I suggest you verify my statements and so far as Flavia is concerned, I doubt if I shall ever be seeing her again. Good-bye.' And with that I put down the telephone.

I was in no great hurry to give up my freedom, although my father was understandably concerned with the succession and, during my last leave, when the subject had arisen, he had told me a most curious story.

He had a very old friend, a Frenchman – the Vicomte de Fontarce – who was a most remarkable man. He owned much land in Upper Egypt, was married and had one beautiful daughter. He told my father that he was determined she should marry me one day and that he would then settle a vast sum of money on her and a million or so would be given to me – all of which pleased my family very much. Alas, the dear girl died after an operation for appendicitis, so that left the Vicomte without anyone to inherit his money.

He hit on a brilliant idea. He asked the French War Office to tell him the names and addresses of at least thirty young war widows who had no children. In due course, he received the information he required, wrote to each of the ladies concerned asking them to send him a photograph of themselves and told them of the following proposition.

Four ladies would be selected. All four would have to live for a year in a closely guarded house in Neuilly and if at the end of that time they had borne him a son, he would give them £100,000 each, they to keep the son for two years after which he would be returned to the Vicomte and they would never see the child again. If they produced a daughter, £50,000 would be the payment and they kept the daughter for life.

In the end, he found himself with one daughter and two sons. The two boys grew up satisfactorily and when later I met them I thought both had a great look of their father.

He treated me very well. When I married in the summer of 1922 he told me that if I had a son he would give me a present of £10,000. Happily, I was able to claim the money when my son was born on 19 January 1924 and he sent me a cheque immediately.

However in the summer of 1919 I was still in search of adventure. Indeed I was sadly green and naif at the time and would have made a ramshackle husband, as the following saga will show. Not long after the Flavia episode I met a very lovely lady called Joan. We became tremendous friends and were soon lovers. When we were not due to meet for a few days, Joan would write me a letter filled with our romance and her expectations of things to come. Unfortunately, she paid little heed to discretion and left a long love-letter to me on her hall table to be posted. Her husband saw it, steamed it open and decided to take a copy. This he sent to his solicitors, requesting that a private detective should be retained to watch our movements.

The next time I was on a week's leave in London, I met Joan for dinner and took her back to our house in Seymour Place – my parents both being in Egypt at the time – and unaware that we were being watched, I returned her to her home in Bruton Street just before dawn.

Two days later I received a telephone call. 'Porchester, this is Frank. I'm ringing to tell you that I know everything about you and my wife. I take a serious view of what has occurred and unless I receive from you a personal cheque for ten thousand pounds by noon on Thursday, I shall start proceedings for divorce and I shall cite you as co-respondent.'

I told him that I did not have ten thousand pounds and if I did, I would not pay it to him.

'We shall see about that,' came his reply. 'You don't know what you're letting yourself in for.'

I was in a panic and suddenly remembered Sir Edward Marshall Hall, a great friend of the family and one of the most eminent KCs in England. I telephoned his office and got an appointment. I went to his chambers and told him my story. He listened attentively with no interruptions. When I had finished, he leaned back in his chair and said, 'My dear boy, the simple answer is this. You will go and see Messrs Theodore Goddard, an excellent firm of solicitors, put yourself in their hands, truthfully telling them the whole story, and do absolutely nothing but what you are told by them. Of course, you will have no communication with this man or his wife. My normal fee for the advice I have given you is five hundred guineas but as I am a friend of your family, I shall only charge you one hundred which you can pay me at your convenience. Now, go and see these solicitors at once. I shall have a word with them and let this be a lesson to you.' I duly did as I was told.

Frank stormed round to Seymour Place in an attempt to see me, but was told by my mother's butler that this was impossible. Eventually, after three days of suspense, he wrote a note in which he said,

> Dear Porchester,
> Unless you pay me ten thousand pounds immediately, you will be cited as co-respondent and it will be a very unhappy ending to your promising career.

I rushed round to Goddard with the note. 'Good heavens,' he said, 'you are damn lucky. This fellow has had the tables turned completely. He will be told by us that he will be in the dock at the Old Bailey for blackmail. You will probably hear no more about it.' This was indeed the case.

The fee for the solicitors' services was four hundred guineas which I did not possess.

I then remembered that Charles Hanbury, who used to be called 'The Dishonourable Charles', was by way of being an entrepreneur in the art world. I went round to see him and told him that my mother had a picture of Emma, Lady Hamilton, by Romney, which I thought she might consider selling. I knew there were a few things in Seymour Place which had been left to my mother by her father, Alfred de Rothschild, which she had said she might not mind selling. This picture was one of them. In due course, Hanbury came round to see the picture and asked what my mother would be likely to accept for it. I mentioned the figure of £80,000. He said he would think about it and would give me an answer in twenty-four hours. He duly came back and asked me to cable my mother with an offer of £75,000. This I did and she cabled back her acceptance, much to the delight of Hanbury and myself.

Foolishly, I wrote to my mother and asked her if she would be very kind and give me one per cent of the £75,000 which would, of course, have more than covered my legal fees and got me nicely out of my predicament. In due course, I got the most awful rocket from my father who wrote saying how staggered he was that any son of his should do such a thing as to ask his mother for commission. He went on to say that he and my mother had been discussing the matter and my mother had been on the point of sending me a cheque for £1,000 when my letter arrived.

I felt more chastened than ever after this and decided to sell something of my own to pay my debts. I also decided that it was time to occupy myself with simpler pursuits. So hearing that the famous horse-dealer, John Drage of Melton Mowbray, had an unusual bargain for sale, I went over to see him. I'd just had my appendix out so was not feeling too strong but felt that as soon as my period of convalescence was over, a good season's hunting would soon set me to rights.

'Look here, m'Lord,' said John Drage, 'I've got just the hunter for you. He's a young chestnut horse and he's only got one fault. He pulls very hard, but that shouldn't worry you.'

'Okay, Mr Drage, it's a deal if I can take him on trial.'

In due course the horse was sent to me and a couple of weeks later I arranged to have a day with the Bramham Moor. A fox was soon found and, weakened somewhat by my sojourn in hospital, I was run away with. After jumping three or four fences out of control, hounds checked and I saw a group milling round a gateway. Unable to stop this wretched animal, I pointed him in their direction. On the fringe, sitting on his horse, was the Mayor of Harrogate. My beast crashed into his quarters, fell and pitched us both into the mud. With hardly enough breath to apologize, I got up covered in mud. Finding my second horseman, I told him to take the first horse back to barracks, climbed aboard my other horse and rejoined the field. We had a good run during the afternoon; killed a fox and, as evening drew near, I suddenly found myself once again in the company of the Mayor of Harrogate. He reined in his horse and eyed me keenly. With the faintest twinkle he said, 'D'you know, a terrible thing happened to me.'

'Did it, Sir?' I said. 'What was that?'

'Well,' he said, 'I think it's very wrong, very wrong indeed and I'm going to write to the Colonel of his regiment. I understand there's a young fella whose name is Lord Porchester and he was riding some horse that ran away with him and, would you believe it, he crashed into my horse, knocked me flying and I might have been badly injured. Mercifully, I wasn't hurt. Don't you think it was shocking?'

Glancing at him anxiously and playing his game I duly replied, 'Yes I do, and I'm most awfully sorry for you. Porchester is a great friend of mine and he's awfully upset about it.'

To which His Worship riposted, 'I hope he's gone home.'

'Oh yes, he's gone home all right.'

'Riding a chestnut horse, wasn't he?'

'Yes, I know the horse, he pulls hard. He's going to get rid of it.'

'Well,' he said, 'when you see him, tell him he must not come out huntin' with an animal he cannot control.'

'I agree, you're absolutely right and it was a maddening thing to have happened. However, if you could feel that you need not write to his Colonel, I'm sure he would be deeply grateful and send you his abject apologies.'

The Mayor thought for a moment or two.

'Oh, I don't think he need do so. After all, you have spoken up very nicely for him and I think we'll leave it at that.'

'That is most kind of you,' I said, raising my hat.

He rode quietly away and I thought this was an object lesson in tactful handling of the young.

When I wasn't hunting, I was racing and whilst still at York I began to visit all the racecourses in the area with my brother officers. This was no new occupation for officers in the 7th Queen's Own Hussars for I could well remember my father often telling me about Lord Marcus Beresford, an ex-7th Hussar, who had spent most of his time haunting racecourses. One time Marcus had strolled over to my father and asked him if he had anything running.

'Yes,' said my father, 'I've a little filly in the first race. She's only a Plater but I think she'll win. She's called False Tooth.'

'Aah!' exclaimed Marcus, 'she'll win all right. You can't stop a false tooth.'

Marcus had the best turn of wit of any man I have ever met. Once when I was alone with him watching a desperate contest between Jack and Solly Joel during the Ham Stakes at Goodwood, he turned to me after a short head finish and said, 'You must remember this race, Porchey. It's not often that you see two Jews fighting for the Ham Stakes.'

One day, after racing at York, one of my brother officers, Donald Pringle, who was very friendly with Gertrude Lawrence, suggested that we might go to London to see her show and take her out to dinner afterwards. This sounded a good idea so I agreed.

Having taken the train from York, we popped into the Cavalry Club for a snack and a half-bottle of champagne before going to the theatre.

'I've told Gertie all about you, Porchey. We'll go backstage and see her when the curtain comes down.'

In due course we struggled through the knot of people at the stage door until we arrived at the star's dressing room.

'Go on, Porchey, she's expecting us, go right in,' and leaning forward, without knocking, he turned the handle of the door and pushed me in first. I stepped in and came to an abrupt halt. With a warning shout from her dresser, I came face to face with the darling of the West End standing before me, absolutely starkers.

She never so much as batted an eyelid. Extending her hand, she walked straight over. 'You must be Lord Porchester. I've heard so much about you from Donald. Do forgive me; now you've seen everything. If you'll give me a moment, I'll slip on some clothes. I'm very much looking forward to dinner.'

Turning, she went behind a screen, leaving me riveted to the spot. What other woman in the world would have the *sang froid* to carry off such a situation?

Gertie's voice floated across from behind the screen. 'Donald, give him a drink, please. You'll find everything you want in the cupboard.'

Twenty minutes later, the charming lady produced a girl-friend for me and we went to the Trocadero for supper *à quatre*. It was a splendid evening in the company of a most delightful person.

It was only a few weeks later that I met the most beautiful Spanish girl I have ever seen in my life. She was La Duchesse Carmen de Peneranda. Unusually, she was a blonde with the most ravishing blue eyes. We had a wonderful month before she had to return to Madrid. Only a short time later I heard that she had gone off with a Spanish bullfighter. I never saw her again: she died of tuberculosis.

After all the excitements and adventures of my life in England, news that my regiment would be returning to India in the coming autumn was most unwelcome. I was bemoaning my fate at White's one evening to Alan Inverclyde, who was ADC to the Governor of Gibraltar, General Sir Horace Smith Dorrien, when he came up with a splendid suggestion.

'My dear Porchey, I've got just the job for you. We need another ADC for the Governor. Shall I put your name forward? There's plenty of polo, racing and fishing; life is good fun on the Rock.'

'What should I have to do?'

'Well, it's a pretty easy life really. Laying on formal dinners, functions and such like.'

'Can one ever get to Spain?' I asked.

'Whenever you feel like it. There's even hunting with the Calpe Hounds.'

'Okay. It sounds good to me . . . that is if my Colonel will release me for a while.'

'I'm sure that can be arranged,' he said.

10
Rock Scorpion

In spite of the fact that my arrival on the Rock took place in the early autumn, it was a truly magnificent day. The air was clear, the buildings white and the towering cliffs impressive. The Governor's barge had come alongside, bearing Lord Inverclyde who walked up the companionway to greet me. The launch, manned by an old Rock Scorpion, as the inhabitants of Gibraltar were called, seemed hardly befitting His Majesty's representative, being rather oily and none too clean.

Alan and I shared a small suite of rooms and presently I was taken down to meet His Excellency, the Governor. Smith Dorrien was very kind, offered sherry and, in due course, introduced his wife. She rather frightened me and I was somewhat relieved when her ladyship returned to Britain.

That evening at dinner, the Governor related one of his favourite stories which he only recounted if he was in a good mood; it concerned his dismissal after the retreat from Mons. At the time the British Army's adjutant-general was Sir William Robertson who had risen from the ranks and during his years of increasing seniority had cultivated no change in his manner of speaking. He invariably dropped his aitches.

The Governor recalled that one day, after the retreat was over, he was in his headquarters, poring over the maps with his other staff officers, when the adjutant-general stalked in, looked at Smith Dorrien and said, ''Ere 'orace, you're for 'ome.'

In many ways the Governor was a remarkable man. Usually extremely kind and courteous, upon occasions he could become irascible to a degree, lose all self-control and work himself up to a frenzy over the smallest trifle. I was shortly to experience one such tantrum. Appointed Master of the Horse, I was responsible for fourteen horses and polo ponies which made up his stable. He used to enjoy hunting on the mainland. But there was one act of courtesy to his rank upon which the Governor was sensitive; namely, the fact that he expected the sentries to salute him whenever he appeared, whether in civilian clothes or in uniform. I had been warned of this by Alan and had tried my best to keep everyone up to the mark.

One morning we walked into Government House and the sentry was either dreaming or did not recognize the Governor. He turned on the man and began to rebuke him with ever-increasing ferocity. He shouted and almost foamed at the mouth. As he strode away, he rounded on me: '... and it's all your fault anyway. You're utterly useless!'

By this time, I was standing rigidly to attention, having quickly decided to hold my tongue. He ranted and raved and then suddenly turned to another tack. '... And as for that horse I rode the other day, she should have been shod the week before. Bloody thing nearly slipped up with me. You're damned incompetent!' And with that he stormed into his room and slammed the door.

Mortified, I retreated to our office and explained all to Alan. He listened attentively with a sly grin spreading slowly across his face.

'Look here, Porchey; I'll lay you a monkey to a mousetrap that within a quarter of an hour he'll send for me and then ask you to go in. He'll offer you the most profuse apologies. You wait and see, but first he's got to simmer down.'

In a quarter of an hour, almost to the minute, the bell in the office rang, which was the signal that Alan was summoned to His Excellency's presence. He winked and some five minutes later returned with a look as much as to say 'I told you so.' I marched in crisply and stood to attention.

'My dear boy, do sit down and have a glass of sherry. I do apologize. I don't know what came over me. You must never pay any attention when I get in such a fury.' He had tears in his eyes and, of course, the apology was far worse than the tantrum.

'What did you think of that sherry? It's a new cask I've just bought. I'd be glad to have your opinion.'

He really was most charming and I became very fond of him.

One day a little domestic difficulty was brought to my attention by the Governor. We kept forty laying hens at the bottom of the garden, whose welfare was tended by an old Rock Scorpion.

'Look here, Porchey,' Smith Dorrien began, 'the cook tells me we are not getting enough eggs. You know how I like 'em for breakfast. What on earth's the matter with the hens? Do you know anything about them?'

'Yes, sir, as a matter of fact I do. I'm very sorry to have to report that our hens seem to have gone into something of a decline. Quite by chance the other day I noticed in a newspaper advertisement an American company advertising some special stuff called "Lay or Bust" and I've sent off for some.'

The Governor roared with laughter. 'Good,' he said, 'glad you're doing something about it. Tell me, what happens if they bust?'

'Well,' I replied, 'if that happens, I shall take full responsibility and I shall replace the hens.'

In due course this special product arrived and our gardener immediately started feeding it to the chickens. Almost miraculously, the egg-count began to go up and the fruits of our combined endeavours began rattling in the nests with such frequency that the operation was proclaimed a marvellous success.

This went on for almost a month until, one morning, the gardener asked if he could have an interview. He came up to the office looking extremely crestfallen.

'Lord, Lord,' he said, 'very, very bad ... cannot say ... very bad.'

'What on earth's the matter?' I enquired of him.

'In night, Lord, in night. Chicken finish ... finish ... all gone.'

'What on earth do you mean? Come on, let's go down and see.'

I led the way to the hen run to find that twenty-eight out of the forty birds had expired in the night.

'What's caused it?' I demanded in horror, knowing H.E.'s fondness for eggs.

'Not understand, Lord. Perhaps your medicine ...?'

'Must have had gunpowder in it or something,' I muttered and retreated hastily to the office. I sent the following cable to my father's stud groom: 'TO WHINCUP HIGHCLERE STUD NEWBURY ENGLAND. OBTAIN FORTY WHITE LEGHORN PULLETS AND DESPATCH FROM SOUTHAMPTON FIRST AVAILABLE SHIP PORCHESTER.'

Life on Gibraltar was not, however, all problems. One morning when we were busy making arrangements for the Governor's Ball, Alan took me into his confidence.

'I've got rather good news. There's a lovely American girl staying at the Reina Christina in Algeciras. Actually she's lived in England for quite a long time but she is travelling with her mother to get over a broken love affair. I've invited them to tea. Do you think you could pop across with the barge and bring them over? The name is Wendell and the daughter is Catherine.'

'Certainly,' I said, 'delighted.'

'I've also suggested that they should come to the ball.'

'Good idea. Where and when do you want me to meet them?'

'At the hotel. Three o'clock sharp.'

In the foyer of the hotel I was told that Mrs and Miss Wendell awaited me in the lounge. Catherine was lovely. She had a beautiful white and pink complexion, gorgeous eyes that danced with merriment and a delicious smile. Wasting no time, I conducted them down to the barge, little realizing at the time that one day Catherine was to become my bride.

On the night of the ball we had one hundred and fifty guests for dinner. Catherine wore a becoming yellow dress and looked quite beautiful. The champagne flowed, the garden was floodlit and the party was a great success.

Shortly after this event, Smith Dorrien sent for me one morning. 'Look here, Porchey, I'm afraid I've got some very bad news. The damned War Office is being forced by the politicians to embark on an economy campaign. I've heard this morning that, in future, I shall have to rely on only one ADC. Alan was here long before you and, therefore, I'm afraid that you will shortly be recalled to your regiment. Of course, I shan't give up without a fight, but I thought I'd better let you know.' Two or three weeks later I received orders to quit my job. I went on leave for two enjoyable weeks at Highclere.

What of the future? My father was in Egypt with Howard Carter looking for the tomb. My mother was still steeped in her nursing home which was continuing to prosper. Now, inevitably, it would mean a return to my regiment in India. Sambo Sewell had hinted that this might be the case before he left, saying, 'We'll miss you, Porchey, don't forget us. We'll need you back as soon as you can escape.'

But whilst on leave in England I was summoned to appear at the War Office to see the Military Secretary. It was an unusual meeting to say the least.

'Look here, Porchester, we've got a job for you to do. It's

a little unusual, but we feel certain that you are the man to handle it.'

'Sounds interesting,' I said guardedly, 'especially if I don't have to go straight back to India.'

'Well, not to put too fine a point on it, we are going to send you to Constantinople, and although you may not like the use of the word, it's to do some spying for us.'

Into my mind flashed the memory of an early dawn and the West Gate of Baghdad.

'It's not spying in the accepted sense. Anyway, er ... we want you to go out there. We shall ask you to take a War Office 'bag' and you will travel by the Orient Express. Time's not too important, two or three weeks from now will do, and then you will report to Colonel Cornwall who is our Military Intelligence Officer attached to General Harrington, the GOC. Do you know him, by any chance?'

'No, sir.'

'Well, he's awfully nice. As a matter of fact, we've decided to give you two cover stories and one of them will be that you are an extra ADC to the General. Now, I'll explain the reason behind all this.

'There are certain situations brewing up in the Balkans and, as you know, your uncle, Aubrey Herbert, is *persona grata* with the Turks. We want to know a bit more of what they're up to and it seemed natural to us that you should go over and make friends with the Sultan, the political figures, the generals, that sort of thing. Our Ambassador, Sir Horace Rumbold, will be able to give you the necessary introductions in order to ease yourself into the diplomatic circle. Your main cover story will be as follows: to the world at large you will be taking over the job of head of the Inter-Allied Passport Bureau. In this office there is a French officer, an Italian and a very small staff, but that's only the cover story. Cornwall will brief you in detail as to your duties and the information we urgently require.' He paused for a moment, watching me closely. 'How does that appeal to you?'

'Sounds very interesting.'

1 The author at Highclere in 1970

2 A portrait of the Fifth Earl of Carnarvon, the discoverer of the tomb of Tutankhamen

3 An aerial view of Highclere

4 A galaxy of racing personalities drawn by B. Villiers in 1929. Lord Carnarvon is on the left of the centré group

5 Lord Carnarvon weighing in after winning the Bibury Welter Plate at Salisbury on Patmos in 1932

6 Tilly Losch: a portrait study by Cecil Beaton in 1939

'We've sent word to your Colonel. Unfortunately, I've no idea how long this will take. Just depends on whether things turn out as we hope. Now, what about your administrative arrangements?'

'May I take my soldier servant?'

'Oh yes, I'm sure that will be all right.'

'Any chance of taking a motor?'

'A motor car?' he echoed. 'Well, I suppose there could be no objection to that. It's not a very big one, is it?'

'Oh no, just a very small car.'

'Okay. Well, tons of luck. Keep in touch. Goodbye.'

And with that we shook hands and I departed.

In due course I found myself on the Orient Express and when I went to my seat it was to find another young officer sitting opposite. He was a Captain in the Irish Guards and introduced himself as Harold Alexander. We soon became fast friends and found we had much in common. Alex had seen tremendous action in France and we spent hours swopping reminiscences of our soldiering careers so far. It transpired that he too was carrying a 'bag' for the Foreign Office. In those days one was supposed to have them padlocked to one's wrist, for it was unthinkable that they should ever be mislaid or stolen.

Alex was a light-hearted companion and we gossiped, dozed and ate until, a few miles outside Sofia, there was a series of shuddering jolts as the front carriages of the train leapt the rails, rocked dangerously but, by the grace of God, came to rest in an upright position. Amidst the hiss of escaping steam, much shouting and gesticulating from the train crew and a thousand enquiries from their passengers, we learned that we must expect anything from two to three days' delay.

Eventually, we reached Constantinople and on the platform I said goodbye to my new-found friend who was one day to become Field-Marshal Lord Alexander of Tunis and lead the British Armies to victory. When we left the train, he was still as immaculate as the moment he had joined it. He struck me as being very handsome and a joy to behold.

11
Turkish Delight

The British, French and Italians were in charge of the occupied zone of Turkey. General Harrington commanded the British troops from his GHQ in the Grande rue de Pera; the Italian forces were under the command of General Mombelli, who was known to every serving British soldier as 'my Belly' and the French were commanded by General Franchet de L'Esperay whom the soldiers called 'desperate Franky'.

Immediately upon arrival, I went to see Tim Harrington who was obviously aware of my mission. He asked me to dinner and explained that he hoped I would have time to actually perform a few tasks as his ADC to which, of course, I agreed. My next move was to introduce myself to the British Ambassador and he in turn arranged for me to meet the various Military Attachés. I was then interviewed by Colonel Cornwall who gave me a detailed and very thorough briefing. I was given a small office in GHQ with one man to assist and I had another office and staff at the Passport Bureau. I also had the enviable distinction of being the only British soldier in the Occupation Forces who was allowed to wear plain clothes at all times.

Very shortly I was moving in the highest social circles with invitations frequently engineered by the British Embassy.

Finally, I had an audience with the ageing Sultan of Turkey, only to find that he was in such poor health, both physical and mental, that nothing could be gained from our meeting.

One of the first assignments I received was to keep an eye on a British Member of Parliament who seemed to have access to all the Turks of note. Imagine my delighted surprise and barely contained mirth when the Colonel gave me the member's name and it was Aubrey Herbert. The following day I met Aubrey at the station and asked him to dine with me that evening at my club, the Cercle D'Orient. I told him that we had to put a 'tail' on him during his stay in Constantinople. He said he thought this was quite normal procedure and that he could well look after himself. He also told me that I would receive details of everything he was doing at all times. Aubrey then went to Hadgi Bekir's shop, where freshly made Turkish Delight was sold daily, and knowing he was being followed, he bought some Rahat Locoum and left by a back door. He then took a circuitous route back to Tokatlians where he was staying. My miserable sleuth had lost him completely for the rest of that day.

One mid-morning, I was sitting in my office in the Passport Bureau when my Italian opposite number, also a cavalry officer and of a good Italian family, suggested that we might have lunch together in one of the local bistros. I agreed and, in due course, he was giving me a very good meal. He was a handsome, nice sort of chap and we got on well. During lunch I realized that he was aware that I had other duties to perform and that at times I took my turn as a cipher officer.

'I hope you won't take this the wrong way but I've got a suggestion to make to you.'

'Yes,' I said, looking at him curiously.

'It is simply this. My people are very anxious to obtain a look at one of your War Office ciphers.'

He looked quite diffident, almost nervous, as well he might in broaching such a subject.

'Good God, are they really?' I parried. 'In what way?'

'Well, we thought you might be able to help us. Our

suggestion is this. If you could tear out one sheet of your cipher, bring it to me at a pre-arranged time, I could have it photographed and the whole operation would take less than ten minutes. Then I'd give it back to you and you could immediately replace it. Nobody would know a thing and we would be most grateful. I have been authorized to suggest that we would be prepared to pay you five thousand pounds in English money the moment you agree to do it and a further five thousand pounds when we have obtained our photograph. How about it?'

Directly I had seen the drift of the conversation, I began formulating a satisfactory reply. After a further brief pause, I looked at him in feigned astonishment.

'My dear chap, only *five thousand pounds*?'

'Well, say ten thousand pounds then?'

'Surely you cannot be serious. *Ten thousand pounds?* Do you really mean to say that your people think I would be willing to become a traitor to my country for a mere ten thousand pounds? They must be joking.'

His eyes were now open wide, desperately trying to read my reactions.

'Do you mean ... do you mean that perhaps if I could obtain a little bit more ... that you might be willing?' he asked me.

Suddenly becoming emphatic I said, 'I should want *double* to even consider the matter.'

He seemed quite relieved. 'Well,' he said, 'I'm not authorized to negotiate such a sum, but between you and me, I have the feeling that our people would be willing. Will you allow me to check?'

'Of course, by all means.'

By now my thoughts were racing ahead.

'Look here,' I said, 'you leave a message for me in the morning. There's no need for us to meet again. Just scribble on a piece of paper "everything okay" should your people agree, and leave it on my desk. Then I will obtain the necessary sheet and make the arrangements to hand it over.'

He was delighted and we had coffee. An hour or two later, I sought out my Colonel.

'Hello, Porchey, how are things going?'

'Splendidly, Sir. Look, I've got something to tell you and I think that I've had a bit of a brainwave.'

I quickly explained the position and then continued: 'As you know, we change our ciphers every month. Now, the constant grouse from the men out here is that we are always terribly short of sporting equipment, footballs, cricket bats and goal posts. Well, if we sold off one of our old cipher sheets, I could pay the twenty thousand quid into our Sports Fund. Think of the equipment we could buy for a sum like that?'

Cornwall rocked with laughter.

'You are priceless, Porchey. What a splendid idea. Come on,' he said, 'I think we ought to go and see the Big White Chief.'

Some ten minutes later we were sitting in front of the GOC. He beamed with delight.

'How could you have thought of it, Porchey. It's a marvellous scheme.'

'One little tiny thought, if I may suggest it.'

'What's that?' he enquired.

'Don't you think it might be advisable to cable the War Office first?'

Tim nodded. 'Yes, we certainly must.'

'Very well, Sir, it's too late today. I'll do it first thing in the morning,' said Colonel Cornwall.

When I went to my office the next day, I found the two magic words scribbled on my note pad 'everything okay'. I was elated and passed the information back to Cornwall.

It was in the late afternoon that the War Office reply came through, naturally enough in cipher. It was not addressed to Colonel Cornwall, but to the GOC himself. It was a literary exercise in abbreviated pent-up fury. 'CANNOT CONCEIVE HOW YOUR PEOPLE COULD SUGGEST SUCH A THING STOP UTTERLY OUT OF THE QUESTION STOP.' Harrington was almost threatened with dismissal. It took him a week or two to recover.

The local political scene was not only complicated by the presence of the French and the Italians, there were also some forty to fifty thousand White Russians of Wrangel's defeated army who had fled from the Caucasus and who were struggling to exist in Istanbul with neither food nor money. Among their number was my old friend General Baratoff who had lost a leg fighting the Bolsheviks. I didn't run into him but I did meet another Russian who fascinated me much more.

I was dining with a brother officer at Tokatlians one evening when I noticed that at a nearby table sat the most ravishing girl with Madonna-like features, oval face and long delicate hands. She looked bored and depressed, hardly speaking to her saturnine companion. From fragments of their conversation, I gathered they were Russian. The evening continued in jovial high spirits until we realized that a fracas was breaking out at the lovely girl's table. The problem was obvious; they could not afford to pay their bill.

After some animated discussion, a Turkish waiter seized upon a solution. His greedy eyes had alighted on the girl's mink stole. With a nonchalant shrug of her shoulders, she flicked it off and allowed him to take it. She seemed quite unperturbed at her loss, treating it in a phlegmatic Russian manner. I was able to glance at the change they received and noticed that it could not have amounted to more than twenty or thirty Turkish liras. The man took the money, shrugged his shoulders and they walked out.

Directly they were clear of the restaurant, I jumped up and went through to find the manager. It was a strict rule at the time that no barter in kind was allowed with the emigré Russians. Producing my identity card, I demanded the return of the stole, pointing out his waiter's infringement of the regulations. He tried to bluff his way out of it.

'No, Sir, I have not got – it was friend of mine.'

'But it was only two or three minutes ago!' I expostulated.

'I know, Sir, but friend has just gone.'

'Very well,' I said sternly, 'I require his name and address and if I don't find him and the stole, this restaurant will be shut down by command of the British Authorities.'

The proprietor was genuinely frightened and gave me an address which turned out to be in the local fur bazaar. Deciding it was unwise to take any action that evening, the following morning, dressed in uniform and accompanied by a Red Cap corporal, I presented myself at the premises. The interview was short and stern. The man protested that he had paid two hundred Turkish pounds.

'Nonsense,' I declared, 'I saw the money on the plate. No meal could have cost the balance in change, even at Tokatlians. I'll tell you what; I have thirty English pounds, you can have them in return for the fur.' He agreed.

My next task was to try to locate my vision of the night before, but I was at a loss as to how to bring this about. Fate treated me kindly. Four nights later, I was dining at a Russian restaurant called the Muscovite, owned and run by emigré Russians. Even the humblest waiter or waitress was nothing less than a prince or princess, but still I could hardly believe my eyes when the girl who came over to take my order turned out to be the erstwhile owner of the mink.

'Have you lost a lovely fur stole?' I enquired innocently.

'Not lost,' she replied, 'it was stolen.'

'Then I've a surprise in store,' I declared triumphantly, 'I happened to be dining at the next table and witnessed the whole sordid transaction. Since then, I have tracked it down and will be delighted to return it to you. Tell me, who was your companion that evening at Tokatlians?'

'He is my husband,' she said, 'but he is no good. He will not work. He has no job.'

'Well, perhaps we could arrange something,' I pondered, just a trifle disappointed. 'Look, this is the address of the Passport Bureau where I have my office. If he'll come up and see me in the morning, perhaps I can give him a job.'

'You are too kind,' she said, her eyes glistening. 'I'll do as you say, but I warn you, he does not like work.'

'What's your name?' I asked.

'Sonya,' she whispered.

Reluctantly, I gave the Russian prince a job cleaning the offices, changing the blotting paper and keeping us supplied with ink. He lasted precisely four days and when I next saw my Russian princess, it was to learn that she had left him. I was overjoyed and immediately suggested that she should move into my quarters in order to teach me Russian.

'But ... but I have a little three-year-old daughter,' she said, fearful that by imparting this news I might lose interest in her.

'Then bring her with you,' I assured her, 'she will be perfectly welcome. I have plenty of room.'

So that she did not become bored, I arranged for Sonya to be trained as a manicurist, for she spoke fluent French and English. She was a captivating creature but she soon posed a number of delicate problems.

Ever since the Ball at Government House, Gibraltar, I had kept up a correspondence with Catherine Wendell and she had now written to say that she would like to visit me in Constantinople. Of all the girls I had met so far, Catherine was the only one I could even begin to see as the future Lady Porchester. The fact that she was an American would not please my father, but I felt certain that her natural grace and charm would soon overcome any resistance and that she would fascinate the rest of the family. So I now had to occupy myself with preparations for her visit. As I was determined to make this a success, I concentrated hard on all the plans I made for her and her mother and it did indeed seem to go extremely well. We had a very carefree time and she ensnared the hearts of everyone, including the Harringtons. Two moments in particular stand out in my mind from her visit.

Tim Harrington had very kindly lent me a horse in order that I could ride out with Catherine. It was a Government charger and on this excursion Maple came along and rode it, while Catherine and I were mounted on my polo ponies. Having been on a good long trek, we came to a stream swollen by the melting snows of the mountains. Whilst not desperately deep, there was a fair race of water and, before risking the crossing with Catherine, I suggested to Maple that he should precede us on the larger animal. He trotted down the bank and began the crossing. We were casually watching his progress when I noticed the horse hesitate and, as he stumbled, Maple flung himself into the stream. The current carried horse and rider downstream while we looked on in horror.

It was a moment for quick decision. I cantered past them and dismounted. In a trice I had tied my hunting crop to my reins and as Maple swept past I hurled it at him. Luckily, he was able to snatch it and I pulled the exhausted man from the water. Such was the paralysing cold of the river that Harrington's charger failed to make either bank and was very soon drowned. We dried off Maple as best we could and I put him on my pony and told him to gallop back. It was a very near thing.

Tim Harrington at first refused to allow me to pay for the horse, saying that it was a natural hazard which the War Office would recognize, but he proved to be wrong. Messages were soon criss-crossing to London, so I gave Tim a cheque for three hundred pounds which he paid to the War Office.

A few nights later the other memorable event of Catherine's visit occurred. Tim's wife was Irish and a lady with a strange sense of humour. On this occasion, they were hosts at an international party for the Diplomatic Corps and I was there in my capacity as ADC. Among the many important guests was General Mombelli, who strutted in full of his own importance. Having exchanged the formal greetings, Lady Harrington beckoned to him to sit down. As he graciously condescended to do so, with a smart tug she whipped the chair from under him.

The portly chap collapsed on the floor to the near hysterical delight of Tim Harrington's wife. 'My belly' was by no means pleased and we were all highly embarrassed. When everyone had got over the shock, I found myself beside the culprit.

'Really,' I whispered, 'you are a naughty girl. Why on earth did you do a thing like that?'

'Oh, but wasn't it funny?'

'Not funny at all,' I remonstrated, 'you might have broken his back.'

Whilst Catherine was still with me, I received two important letters both of which had considerable bearing on my plans for my future. One was from the regiment suggesting, in the nicest possible way, that it was high time I returned to India and that if I did I would become adjutant in the autumn, and the other was from Dick Dawson.

Just before I had left Highclere for Constantinople, Dick Dawson had told me that his brother Sam had acquired a brown colt foal by Swynford out of Blanche, bred at the National Stud by old Harry Greer. He had suggested that as this yearling which they owned would probably sell for a very small sum at the forthcoming December Sales, he might suit me very well. I had told him to go up to two thousand guineas for the colt as I had been left twenty-five thousand by Alfred de Rothschild.

'Good Lord,' Dick had said, 'we shall probably get him for seven to eight hundred. He has not got the best of legs but it's worth taking a chance, so I shall buy him for you.'

Imagine my fury when I received a long letter from Dick explaining that his irascible brother Sam had run across to him when he heard the yearling knocked down to Dick and had said, 'How right you were, my dear Dick, to buy him in for us. We could never have let him go for such a ridiculously low figure.'

Dick promptly stated that he had bought him for me. Sam screamed and raged, insisting that Dick had bought him and that they would race him in partnership. Weakly Dick agreed and I lost Blandford. My whole life would have taken on a completely different hue had this tragedy not occurred.

Dick's letter made me think that I might as well stay in the regiment for a bit longer so that when, just before Catherine was due to depart, I received a letter from Sambo Sewell asking me to confirm my acceptance of appointment as adjutant, I wrote immediately accepting. At the same time I asked Catherine to become my wife.

In order to allow sufficient time for our marriage in England, I suggested to Sambo that before embarking for India, I should go to the Cavalry School at Netheravon. He agreed and I returned to England.

Before my father approved the match, and obviously with a mind to the success he had achieved with Alfred de Rothschild, he counselled me as follows: 'It seems to me totally unnecessary to go marrying an American and, if what you tell me is correct, even more ridiculous to marry one with no money. If you are determined to do such a thing, I would have thought it much better to have picked a very rich one. You'll find that love in a cottage is very dreary. I can only tell you that before I consented to marry your mother, I got hold of Alfred de Rothschild and made some very stringent terms before the event took place. However, Henry, I suppose I'd better have a look at this young lady so perhaps you will bring her along to luncheon.'

When eventually I did take Catherine to lunch, it was at Seymour Place. At the end of the meal, when I was alone with my father, his comment was direct and to the point: 'She's not bad – quite good-looking.' Although my mother was very non-committal, I thought the lunch had turned out reasonably well.

As an engagement ring for Catherine, Cartiers reset the square-cut sapphire given by my father to Prince Victor, my godfather, who in turn had bequeathed it to me in his will. My father had acquired it for four hundred pounds. I had it valued after it was reset and was advised a figure of two thousand, five hundred. Now it must be worth all of ten thousand pounds and one day I hope it will go to Penelope, our daughter.

On 17 July 1922 Catherine and I were married at St Margaret's, Westminster. As I was only mid-way through my course at Netheravon, there was no chance of a honeymoon so we spent the week-end at Highclere. Dickie Mountbatten, a life-long friend, had come to our wedding with Edwina but we were unable to go to theirs as it took place the very next day, also at St Margaret's.

The night before our wedding, I had thrown a stag party at the Cavalry School at which one fellow officer got so drunk that he jumped through a window, while another nearly drowned in the Avon. My brother officers gave me a beautiful silver salver as a wedding present and their names remain as deeply etched in the metal as they are in my memory. When I read them today, I find I am the sole survivor.

My father's gift to Catherine was a diamond tiara which was a family heirloom. It was reset as a bandeau by Cartier and valued for insurance at that time at thirty thousand pounds. My father was somewhat depressed all that summer, not by our wedding, but because his concession to dig in the Valley of the Kings at Luxor was drawing to a close. The last season's work had been completed, nothing had been found and only a few square yards of the Valley now remained to be excavated by Howard Carter in the autumn.

However it was on 6 November that Carter's cable arrived and with its receipt all gloom vanished. It was the prelude to triumph: 'AT LAST HAVE MADE WONDERFUL DISCOVERY IN VALLEY STOP MAGNIFICENT TOMB WITH SEALS INTACT STOP RECOVERED SAME FOR YOUR ARRIVAL CONGRATULATIONS HOWARD CARTER.' On 30 November *The Times* splashed the following headline sent by their Cairo correspondent from the Valley of the Kings by runner to Luxor: 'An Egyptian Treasure. Great find at Thebes. Lord Carnarvon's long quest.'

My father immediately set sail for Egypt with my sister

and we, in company with the rest of the world, waited anxiously to learn whether or not Howard Carter and my father had succeeded. They returned with wondrous news and in London the Court Circular announced that the King had received Lord Carnarvon in audience at Buckingham Palace and listened with great interest to a description of the important discoveries made recently by him and Mr Howard Carter at the culmination of the excavations which they had carried on for nearly sixteen years and that Lord Carnarvon had assured the King of his confident expectation that still further objects of great importance would be found when the third sealed chamber, believed to be the actual tomb of Tutankhamen, was opened.

No sooner had my father returned than I had to leave for India. I just had time to hear about his discoveries before saying good-bye. I decided to leave behind my three-legged terrier Susie as she had become devoted to my father during the war when I had been abroad and now she always slept by his bed. (She had lost her leg when she was knocked down by a taxi in Berkeley Square.) All in all it seemed best to leave her where she was happiest.

On Christmas Day 1922 Catherine and I embarked at Tilbury.

12
The Curse

Returning to India was like putting the clock back a full half-century. For all the change in military tactics, the First World War might never have occurred. True, there was violent discussion on the rival merits of the tank and the horse, but India still basked in the reflected glory of the Imperial Crown and our enemies were the North West tribesmen. Life soon settled down to parties, pig-sticking and polo. It was an insulated world where gentlemen were expected to be gentlemen and one and all lived for the regiment. For us, life was gay and secure.

We had not been there long before Herbert Fielden, captain of our polo team, asked me to play Number Two in the final of the Inter-Regimental between the 7th and 11th Hussars. It took place one warm, still afternoon in 1923 at the Wheeler Polo Ground, Meerut, in the United Province of India, after the worst heat of the day had passed.

On a raised and canopied dais the Viceroy, Lord Reading, and his guests, including Lord Inchcape, Chairman of the P & O Line, were enjoying the thrills of a close-run game. It was almost 4.30 p.m.; the scores were level and we were playing the very last chukka. In the remaining few seconds, a brief opportunity occurred and, with a push rather than a stroke,

I managed to hit the ball toward the goal. It caught the wicker of the goalpost then, more by luck than good management, trickled over the line.

Our team, hot and thirsty, were presented to the Viceroy, Fielden receiving the cup and each of us a commemorative trophy. It was just after I had shaken hands with His Excellency that a member of the Viceroy's Bodyguard stepped forward. He was a handsome Sikh, dressed in white and wearing the scarlet Viceregal sash. He came across to where I was standing and, saluting, said, 'Sahib, a priority telegram from Egypt.' He handed it to me, saluted again and retreated.

Turning to the Viceroy, I asked permission to open the cable. 'Certainly. I hope it's not bad news about your father.'

I tore the envelope open and read the following: 'FROM SIR JOHN MAXWELL COMMANDER-IN-CHIEF EGYPT TO SIR CHARLES MUNROE C-IN-C INDIA URGENT PLEASE EXPEDITE AN IMMEDIATE PASSAGE FOR LORD PORCHESTER TO CAIRO WHERE HIS FATHER IS VERY SERIOUSLY ILL.' Typed beneath the message, which had been re-directed from my regimental HQ were the words: 'Three months' compassionate leave granted.'

Lord Reading murmured, 'I'm so sorry,' and Lord Inchcape, standing at his side, immediately made a helpful suggestion: 'The *Narkunda* sails tomorrow and will be calling at Suez. I know she is full to the gunwales but I shall instruct her Captain to have an officer's cabin made available. I shall also tell him to make maximum speed, the expenses of which,' he murmured as an aside, 'I shall naturally defray, in order that you can get to your father's bedside as soon as is humanly possible.'

Then it was the turn of Lord Reading: 'I also have a suggestion.' He turned to one of his ADCs. 'I've an idea we ought to put Porchester on my train and send him down to Bombay tonight. He will then have sufficient time in the morning without any fear of missing the sailing.'

The ADC agreed, but added, 'Perhaps I could suggest

that instead, we couple your personal coach to the Punjab Express. It'll reach Bombay by seven in the morning.'

'Excellent,' said the Viceroy.

I returned from the polo field to the Wheeler Club where Catherine and I were staying. I told her to pack up our belongings in Mhow, sell the polo ponies and join me, in due course, either in Cairo or in England. She started to cry and said she could not bear leaving me but I told her that her many friends would look after her when she got back to our bungalow. I had an intuitive feeling that I would not be returning to India. A telegram such as I had received seemed to indicate an illness of great severity. I felt desperately sad that my father should be so ill at this moment of triumph.

We reached Aden in record time having averaged nearly twenty-three knots. The chairman of the P & O had arranged for the Arab coolies to be double banked so that we coaled in eight hours instead of about twenty-four. There again, Lord Inchcape defrayed this considerable expense, which was most generous of him. At Suez, a launch came alongside with Sir John Maxwell's ADC and we were soon streaking across the harbour to the railway siding, at which stood Sir John's private train. Conkie Maxwell warned me that we might be too late as apparently my father had nearly passed away the previous night. By two o'clock that afternoon I had reached the Continental Hotel.

I was not to know at the time that many months previously, my father, who had always been interested in spiritualism and the study of the occult, had received a letter from a man whose name was Count Hamon and who was extremely well known in society circles as the clairvoyant, Cheiro. Upon the news of the discovery of the tomb he had written to my father warning him not to become involved. This matter preyed on my father's mind and he decided to consult his own clairvoyant, Velma.

Velma was a seer and palmist, famed for many predictions including the assassination of the Tsar of Russia and his son,

Alexis Nicolaevitch, and the death of Francisco Pancho-Villa, the bandit and Mexican president, whose hand he had read on the outskirts of Mexico City. Possibly one of the most significant recorded prophecies he made was to the Duchess of York, now, of course, HM Queen Elizabeth the Queen Mother. He met her at an Elizabethan pageant in aid of charity at Hatfield, the ancestral home of the Cecils. Velma had been provided with a booth in the Elizabethan gipsy encampment and the young Duchess, accompanied by some friends, arrived at his stall and laughingly held out her hand. The Line of Life showed on both hands, strong and clear, indicating long life. A line extending from the Mount of Venus to that of Mercury indicated great capacity for loyalty and affection. The Line of Saturn started from the Life Line, indicating good fortune through personal merit. The Head Line was joined to the Life Line, sharply left it, and proceeded directly to the Mount of the Moon without interruption. This indicated good sense, clear and strong willpower.

'Then you consider that I have a very good hand?' enquired the Duchess with a smile. 'Is that all you have to tell me?'

'Well, your Royal Highness,' Velma replied, 'there are several other features which are all of good omen, but it is difficult for me to speak to you about it in detail.'

'Do tell me if it is anything really interesting,' the Duchess begged.

Velma looked hard at the palm again.

'I see by indications on the various lines and mounts of your hand that your marriage, so happy and successful, will be made more successful still by the arrival of a child who will be worshipped from one end of the empire to the other.'

When he read my father's hand, Velma found a fairly long Life Line, but thin in the centre, where there was an ominous spot which – given other combinations in the hand – might indicate death. Unfortunately, it seemed that the confirming signs were there also, for there was a spot at the junction of the Lines of Heart and Apollo.

'I see great peril for you,' he confided to my father.

My father had made a spirited, in-character reply. 'Whatever happens, I shall see to it that my interest in things occult never gets so strong as to affect either my reason or my health.'

However, before making his final visit to Egypt, my father had again visited Velma. To the palmist's considerable surprise, he noticed that the ominous spots to which he had previously referred looked, if anything, as if they had increased in intensity. In particular, the spot on the Life Line seemed perilously close to the Earl's present age.

'If I were you,' he suggested quietly, 'I should make some public excuse and finish. I can only see disaster ahead.'

'That is out of the question,' my father had replied. 'I must finish what I have begun.'

When I arrived at the Continental Hotel, it was to find that my mother, in company with Dr Marcus Johnson, had courageously flown in a tiny Puss Moth right across Europe and over the Mediterranean in order to be at my father's bedside.

I went upstairs and found that my mother, sister and Marcus were all asleep. I asked one of the nurses on duty whether I could see my father.

'I'm afraid he is delirious at the moment,' the nurse replied. 'Actually, your mother said she would like to take you in herself.'

'Don't worry, I'll go in now.'

I followed the nurse into the bedroom. There lay my father, unshaven, with bloodshot eyes and yellow foam flecking his lips. A pulse in his throat seemed to twitch in irregular spasms. I took his hand.

'Papa, this is Henry. I have come to make you better.'

My father turned his head and stared at me. His reaction was quite extraordinary.

'Do you remember how those Italians ran like rabbits on the Piave?'

I looked at him in astonishment. He had never been in the

army. For a second or two I was nonplussed and then said, 'Yes, indeed they did.'

My father continued, 'We ought to have shelled them and shot them like rabbits...'

Again at a loss for words, I hastily agreed with him. Turning round and catching the eye of the nurse, her expression seemed to indicate 'take no notice, he is completely delirious'.

I stood looking down at him, filled with sadness and remorse for all those wasted years when we had known so little of each other. I had travelled thousands of miles only to find that he was now beyond my reach. I could count on one hand the number of occasions upon which we had enjoyed real affection and companionship.

What an extraordinary man he had been. Frail in health, yet an adventurer who had travelled far. A man with the widest possible interests ranging from spiritualism to politics, an excellent photographer, one of the best shots in Europe, an owner of racehorses and a breeder of good bloodstock. Now he had added archaeology to his long list of accomplishments.

Later in the evening I was reunited with the family and Howard Carter. It was he who told me what had happened:

> Your father had a little mosquito bite which he nicked with his cut-throat razor, but it seemed to have no significance at all. He put some iodine and cotton wool on it and thought no more of it. That evening, he told your sister that he felt he might have a chill coming on. When Eve took his temperature it was a hundred and one but, by morning, it had returned to normal.
>
> Your father then felt quite well enough to come out to my house but, that evening, seemed to take a turn for the worse and when your sister found that his temperature had risen to a hundred and one again, she decided forthwith to take him to Cairo. It was the best thing she could have done.
>
> He was apparently quite comfortable and received all

the medical attention available. It was obvious that he had contracted blood poisoning but after ten days the worst seemed over, so much so that he was able to sit up for a few hours in the daytime. I am afraid that must have caused his final relapse, because, during the night, he became seriously ill and Johnny diagnosed virus pneumonia.

That night I decided to retire early and, after another brief visit to my father's room, I prepared for bed and out of habit placed my torch on my bedside table. It seemed that my head had no sooner touched the pillow than I became aware of a knock on the door. I glanced at my watch which read five to two and called, 'Come in.'

It was one of the nurses.

'Lord Porchester, your father has passed away. Your mother has just closed his eyes and she would like you to go in and hold his hand while it is still warm and say a prayer with her.'

Snatching my dressing gown and running a comb through my hair, I picked up my torch and went out into the corridor. As I began to hurry towards my father's room, the lights in the passage suddenly went out and the whole hotel was plunged into darkness. Switching on my torch, I continued on my way. I handed the torch to one of the nurses and told her to get some candles from the manager's office.

Going into my father's room, I found Almina on her knees. Kneeling down beside her, I took my father's hand and prayed silently. A few moments later I left the room. As I did so, the lights in the hotel went on again, some five minutes after their failure.

With a heavy heart, I walked back along the corridor. I slept fitfully and awoke early to the sudden realization that my name was no longer Porchester but Carnarvon. As I dressed, it dawned on me that my soldiering days must come to an end and with them a life of comparative freedom. However, my first task would be to take my father's body home for burial.

I went along to breakfast and saw Howard Carter sitting alone. He looked as if he had not slept and was reading the three main Cairo newspapers which were printed in Arabic.

'You'll notice that the news of your father's death has been recognized by a black mourning band round all the papers. He was very much loved here in Egypt, more so, of course, since we found the tomb.'

Carter resumed his reading and suddenly stiffened with apparent irritation.

'Oh, these people! I don't know if you were aware of it, but last night there was an electricity failure...'

'As a matter of fact, I was,' I replied, 'because, at the time, I was walking down the corridor to my father's room.'

'Well, the newspapers have concocted a story that the lights were put out by the express command of King Tut. They say, in effect, that your father, an infidel, had ignored all the warnings and disturbed the sacred remains of King Tutankhamen. To uphold his sovereignty, the King has taken his vengeance and, in order that all should note his displeasure, he turned out every single light in the city of Cairo at the moment your father passed away.'

I responded to Carter's mood but shortly had cause to think again when I was handed a message with a request from Lord Allenby that I should visit him at the residency at ten o'clock. Arriving five minutes before the appointed time, I was immediately ushered into his room. Allenby came forward.

'How very good of you to come. I am most terribly sorry about the passing of your father. It must have been an awful blow. I'm only grateful that you managed to reach Cairo in time. I asked you to come over because I felt we owed you some explanation for the story that has appeared in the morning press. I have to admit that it is quite extraordinary. However, I am going to introduce you to the head of the Cairo Electricity Board who is waiting outside.'

The man came in and told me the following story. 'I was in bed and was wakened by a telephone call from one of my duty officers. He told me there had been a complete power failure throughout the city but he had no idea as to what had caused the total black-out. It was 2 a.m. and he asked me to come immediately. I threw on some clothes and had just got into my car when, to my surprise, all the lights in Cairo went on again. We have four zones, north, south, east and west, and I went to each of them in turn. All told me they could not find any reason for this failure and there is no technical explanation for it whatsoever.'

My next job was to arrange to have my father embalmed before taking him home. However, Carter wanted me to visit Luxor in order to have a look at the tomb and I agreed that I would once I had found a suitable ship and made all the arrangements for returning to England. This turned out to be far more difficult than I had envisaged. Sailors are a superstitious crowd and most captains will do everything possible to avoid taking a coffin on board their vessel. In due course, however, arrangements were completed and, having visited the tomb, I returned to Cairo and embarked for England.

My father had expressed the wish that he should be buried in a coffin made of Highclere oak and that neither headstone nor anything else should mark his last resting place. I chose a spot on Beacon Hill, as he had asked that his grave should be sited so that he could look over the stud farm he loved so well and see into his bedroom window. The Bishop of Winchester consecrated the ground and the funeral took place in the presence of my mother, my sister and myself, and some of his devoted retainers.

The funeral service was marred by a small aeroplane, carrying a photographer from the *Daily Express*, flying low over the grave taking pictures of my mother kneeling at the graveside. I thought this very bad taste and later, when I remonstrated with Max about it, he shrugged his shoulders and replied tersely, 'Your father was hot news.'

Shortly after I returned to Highclere, I learned that another death had occurred. The housekeeper at Highclere was a very charming old Scottish lady and she told me of the death of my little fox terrier bitch called Susie. You will remember that my father adored her; he always asked Mrs McLean to look after her while he was abroad and she slept in her basket in Mrs McLean's bedroom.

According to her, at five minutes to four on 5 April 1923, Susie sat up in her basket, howled like a wolf and fell back dead. (There is, of course, two hours' difference between Cairo time and London time.) Mrs McLean felt that this curious story seemed to confirm what she had read about the alleged curse that had been put upon my poor father.

By now the newspapers of the world had caught on to the idea of the curse. It did not matter how many times Howard Carter refuted the claim that somewhere on the golden shrine appeared those now famous words 'Death shall come on swift wings to him who disturbs the sleep of the Pharaoh'. No such inscription existed in the tomb. The public fervour on the matter became so intense that Howard Carter was forced to issue a statement.

> It has been stated in various quarters that there are actual physical dangers hidden in Tutankhamen's tomb – mysterious forces, called into being by some malific power, to take vengeance on whomsoever should dare to pass its portals. There was, perhaps, no place in the world freer from risks than the tomb. When it was opened, scientific research proved it to be sterile. Whatever foreign germs there may be within it today have been introduced from without...

However, even Howard Carter was not immune from mysterious circumstances. He owned a canary which lived in a cage in his bungalow at El Gurnah and brought joy to the archaeologist in his lonely hours. His house servants used to place the cage outside in order that the bird might enjoy an airing. On one occasion, shortly after my father's death, it had been trilling to its heart's content when suddenly, it fell silent. Carter's manservant, noting the cessation of song, rushed outside to see what had happened. He saw, swaying on its coils and standing erect, a jet black cobra in the very act of swallowing its prey. The sacred cobra in ancient Egypt was guardian of the king.

The news spread like wildfire, to such effect that an important official of the Egyptian government brought the famous snake-charmer Mussa, to the valley. This man went to the tomb – some considerable distance from Carter's bungalow – and drew from it both another cobra and a grass snake. How they arrived there no-one knew, but certain it is that this incident added fuel to the fire of the current superstition.

A week or two later, at Highclere, I received a telephone call. A lady was on the other end of the line.

'Lord Carnarvon?' she enquired. 'You won't know me at all, but I am a spiritualist and worked very closely with your father. In fact, at our seances, I acted as his medium.'

'Oh, how interesting,' I replied.

The lady continued, 'But far more important than that, I have to tell you that I had a message from your father two days ago.'

'Really,' I murmured.

'Yes, we had a very long conversation and he has asked me to pass on to you an instruction. It is that on no account whatsoever should you ever step inside the tomb of King Tutankhamen again. Under no circumstances,' she repeated with emphasis. 'This is the express wish of your father and he asked me to tell you. He pointed out that if you disobey this order you will surely die and this would mean an end to the House of Herbert for, as yet, I understand you have no children.'

Not really knowing quite what to say, I thanked the lady and told her I would be happy to carry out my father's wishes. What else could I say? The whole thing was quite extraordinary: the lights in Cairo, the death of my bitch and the fact that I had attended at least two seances which my father had held at Highclere Castle. These he used to conduct in East Anglia bedroom.

I had watched Helen Cunliffe-Owen put into a trance on an occasion when Howard Carter had also been present. It had been an eerie, not to say unpleasant, experience which had shaken me considerably. One moment she had been her normal self, the next her features had become strained and white. Suddenly she had started talking in an unknown tongue which, to everyone's astonishment, Howard Carter had pronounced as being Coptic. On another occasion, I had actually seen flowers levitate from a bowl and I remembered particularly one seance when my sister had been placed in a trance. It was for these reasons that however sceptical I might have been, I could not dismiss the matter out of hand.

Some weeks later I received a further telphone call – the last of its kind.

'Lord Carnarvon, I hate to disturb you, but your father came through again last night. He asked me if I had passed on his message and whether you had acquiesced. I answered both questions in the affirmative. He said how pleased he was and sent his love.'

As it happens, I have never returned to the tomb which I had found cold and uninteresting and I had no desire to see it again. Whereas I am not superstitious, I am on record as having said that I would not enter the tomb again for one million pounds. But I must confess that, in these hard times, were the offer to be made, I would be sorely tempted to accept.

13
Sorrows of Succession

It was not until we laid my father to rest on Beacon Hill that I really appreciated the fact that I had inherited Highclere. Under the law of primogeniture I inevitably inherited the estates and I had felt certain that my father would have ensured the future of these so when I received a letter from Molony, our family solicitor, inviting me to attend his office in the City, I did so without any fear. I was about to receive a severe shock.

He told me that my father had made one or two codicils which he did not consider should be contested, otherwise everything, all his personal estate with the exception of a silver Fabergé cigarette case and his watch, had been left to my mother. I had always taken the keenest interest in everything to do with the stud farm but as my mother had been left all the bloodstock, this made matters extremely difficult for me. I had no assets which could be realized to pay the death duties.

My trustees suggested to me that Highclere would have to go and that I should either buy or build a little house, selling off the land and perhaps keeping the stud farm. I said very little. I loved Highclere where I had been brought up with Eve and I was damned if I was going to part with my inheritance without a struggle.

I returned to Highclere in a very sombre mood and as the car swung through the lodge gates, which were opened by the lodge-keeper, it occurred to me that much would have to change. However, looking out of the window at the park and the trees that had stood there for centuries, I made the decision that nothing would force me to part with Highclere.

My days in the army, of course, came to an end and I resigned my commission, as I had to give all my time to keeping the estate going. This was a very difficult procedure as I only had nine months' grace before paying death duties without attracting interest.

I contacted Joe Duveen, the greatest international art dealer of that day, and asked him to come and buy any of my pictures that he fancied: this would help me to pay the death duties. He duly arrived and asked for a pair of steps and a powerful torch. I explained the position to him and he told me he had had to do this sort of job on many occasions.

'I was fond of your father,' he said, 'and, therefore, will do all I can to help, but I want you to remember one thing – there is no friendship in business. Joe Duveen has always had one maxim and that is Joe Duveen only deals for one hundred per cent profit.'

He did particularly well out of one picture called *The Woodgatherers* by Sir Joshua Reynolds. For that he only gave me £10,000 as he said it would be a complete gamble whether or not the painting could be restored. He told me that if it could, he would probably get anything between £60,000 and £100,000 for it and that if I liked to have a go at having it restored myself, I was very welcome to do so. Cowardly creature that I was, I let him buy it for £10,000. It was beautifully restored and he sold it in America for £70,000.

One incident during his visit still stands out in my memory. We were looking at a full-length picture of the Earl of Chesterfield and its companion picture of the

Countess, by Thomas Gainsborough. The Earl was dressed in a red suit, with his English collie dog looking up at him and his right hand holding a shepherd's crook. His wife was depicted in a lovely blue dress and both pictures were very attractive. Duveen clambered up the steps and examined both of them closely. Climbing down, he paused for a moment or two.

'Yep,' he said, 'they're all right. Now, let me see; I'll give you ... I'll give you,' he paused, '... £25,000 for the lady and ... £17,000 for the Earl.'

I thought this very strange and said, 'Tell me, why do you offer a lower price for the picture of the Earl?'

'Well, you can think it out for yourself. Everyone who is normal likes looking at a beautiful woman, but they don't get anything like the enjoyment out of a man standing alone. That's why the price is disproportionate.'

By the end of the morning, I had agreed to sell him eight pictures including, of course, *The Woodgatherers*. I was very sad to lose them.

Having denuded the walls of Highclere of the most valuable paintings with which I could part, it became the turn of the pearls which still can be seen decorating the throat of the first Countess of Carnarvon in her portrait by Van Dyck. I collected them from the bank and having absolutely no idea as to their value, I made my way to Tessiers. Herbert Parsons was an old friend and when I placed them carefully on the black velvet pad, he looked at them and murmured, 'At first blush, unloved for centuries. I imagine you've insured them?'

'As a matter of fact I have not.'

'Then do so for £50,000 and I'll tell you what I'd like you to do. Will you give them to your sister and ask her to wear them for a week to ten days and then bring them back to me and I'll tell you what I think of them.'

I knew Eve would do me this favour and I was sure that her skin would be very good for them. When I took them back ten days later, they were lustrous and radiating life.

'There, what did I tell you,' he exclaimed when he saw them. Now we can get down to work. Firstly, I must unstring them and weigh them. I'll have them restrung and if you'll call round in a couple of days, I'll give you my opinion as to their value. At first glance they seem beautifully matched.'

I returned the following week.

'Here are your pearls. You will see that I have polished up the clasp and carefully restrung them.'

'They look marvellous,' I agreed.

'Now, the first thing I have to say to you is that I don't wish to buy them. As you know, silver is my business and pearls are not, but I am going to tell you what to do.' He paused reflectively. 'If you are hungry, really hungry, and you are being forced to sell them don't take less than £45,000. If you're not all that desperate, a fair price commercially is £50,000; on the other hand, if you can find someone who actually wants to buy them, then ask £55,000.'

'I see,' I replied.

'As you probably know, Paris is the hub of the world's pearl market and I would suggest that you take them to France. That is where the big deals are done and where you are most likely to find your buyer. Do you happen to have any contacts over there?'

'Well, I know Jacques Cartier pretty well.'

'Excellent, you're made. You couldn't do better. Put them in your pocket and take them to Jacques.'

Telling Catherine what I was going to do and as she was already pregnant and not fit to travel, I took the Golden Arrow and went to the Ritz. Telephoning Jacques Cartier, I explained my mission.

'Certainly I'll come round and have a look, but I'm terribly busy and it will not be until seven-thirty this evening.'

'That's fine,' I agreed. 'Look forward to seeing you.'

When, in due course, I showed the pearls to Cartier, his reaction was immediate.

'*Elles sont belles! Elles sont très belles!*'

'They *are* very beautiful,' I agreed with him.

'Do you have them insured?' he asked.

'Of course.'

'Very well, I shall take them to my shop and weigh them.'

'That has already been done, my dear Jacques, here are the details.'

'Aha,' he said, looking at me with a glint in his eyes, 'and how much are you expecting, because I believe I *may* have a client.'

'£55,000,' I replied.

'Oo la la! Oo la la!' he exclaimed. '*Alors*, okay; but I must, of course, weigh, measure and check them to be satisfied they are as good as I believe.'

He brought them back the following evening and over a bottle of champagne he told me he had an Indian client who was anxious to acquire them. Apparently, he wished to wear them in his turban the following year at the Delhi Durbar.

'Fifty-five thousand?'

'Fifty-five thousand, Jacques, and no bargaining.'

'Oh, you are a very hard man, my dear Porchey.'

'Not at all,' I replied, 'you know as well as I that the pearls are worth it.'

'I agree. Now, if this deal does come off with my Indian Maharajah it will mean, I presume, that £50,000 will be paid to you and £5,000 to Messrs Cartier?'

'No fear,' I replied, 'Messrs Cartier can get what they like. I don't mind how much you make, but I must get £55,000 net. Surely to an Indian Prince such a sum would be peanuts. And, by the way, for your information, although you will make out your cheque to me, the money is destined to go to our Chancellor of the Exchequer.'

I made it plain to Jacques that I would deal with no-one but Messrs Cartier and it was up to him to make whatever arrangements he pleased with the Maharajah and, as I could not delay my return to London, he must bring me the cheque the following day. The deal was done without further argument and I telephoned Catherine to tell her the good news.

'Well done, my darling,' she enthused, 'are you being a good boy?'

'A good boy! I've had no time to be anything but good. However, I'm going out on the town tonight to celebrate and I'll see you tomorrow.'

I was a little late arriving at the Gare du Nord in the morning and hurried to catch the train. Seeing a porter, I handed him a franc and asked him to buy the continental edition of the *Daily Mail*. He did so and brought it to me. Two minutes later, when the train began to move, I picked up the newspaper and glanced at the front page: 'First cultured pearls appear from Japan'.

In this instance I had prevailed in a photo-finish, for within a few hours the value of my pearls had plummeted to something approaching £3,000.

At Highclere, economy was the rule of the day and I set about cutting the staff to what I believed then to be the minimum necessary for the running of the house. We ended up with my butler and valet, a first footman, second footman, a hall boy, an usher, a head chauffeur and a second chauffeur, a chef, a first kitchen maid, a second kitchen maid, a scullery maid and a still-room maid, a housekeeper, five housemaids, an electrician, a nightwatchman, a head groom and two other grooms.

Always an early riser, I rode out each morning round the park. This brought about the first sign of friction.

My agent, James Rutherford, was a difficult Yorkshireman in his late sixties who had worked for my father for many years. However, he had been given a free hand during a period when it was not necessary for the estate to produce a profit. Now the situation was very different. It is always difficult to teach an old dog new tricks if not impossible. The Major was a taciturn man and bitterly resented any remark or question which he would regard either as a veiled criticism or a reflection on how he went about his work. For instance, I might say, 'What do you think about that plantation on Siddown Hill?'

To which he would reply with some asperity.

'Well, what about it? I heard that you were at the Saw Mill early yesterday morning and you asked Frank Soper what he thought. I do wish you would come and ask me if you want to know anything. I'm your agent. Don't talk to the men.'

He was steeped in the old ways, whereas I, after more than seven years in the army, was used to dealing with men direct. So after several tiffs, it became obvious that he and I could not work together and I sent for him to come to my room.

'Now look here,' I said, 'this situation cannot continue. We don't work well together and I'm afraid the time has come when we must part company.'

'Does that mean you are giving me the sack?'

'Well,' I said, 'call a rose by any other name, but the answer is yes it does.'

'Huh!' he grunted, 'I imagined it would end up like this. I'm only sorry I didn't resign on the death of your father. How much notice have I got?'

'Six months.'

There was no more to be said so he got up and left.

Then I made a great mistake. I offered the job to his son, but this arrangement proved, in a very short time, to be a complete failure and in due course, I had to find another agent.

I had not long inherited my estates when I heard that my mother was contemplating a second marriage. This upset me as such a short period had elapsed since my father's death.

My mother and father had both been close friends of Dorothy Dennistoun who had been married to Ian Dennistoun, one-time colonel in the Grenadier Guards. However, they were by now divorced. One day Dorothy telephoned my mother: 'Almina darling, I hear you're going to Paris. Could you be an angel and deliver a letter to Ian?' Almina agreed and on arrival at the Ritz, sent a message to the Colonel suggesting that he might like to join her for dinner. Having seen photographs of Dorothy's ex-husband, she was horrified at the apparition that appeared: with sunken eyes, drawn cheeks and shabby clothes, he was a picture of misery. Almina was overcome by pity and nothing he required was to be denied. First, he must have a brand-new wardrobe and move into the Ritz.

Dennistoun had been living as the guest of two little French midinettes and they had given him at least one square meal per day for about two years. To his eternal shame, he never even thanked them for what they had done or informed them of where he was about to live.

Undoubtedly, Almina and Tiger Dennistoun were genuinely attracted to one another and were eventually married in a registry office. For more than a decade she cared for him and this was the beginning of her financial ruin. Tiger was a very sick man and my mother extremely extravagant. First she bought a house in Scotland, spending about three hundred thousand pounds on it. After a year it was sold at a fraction of its cost and she bought another house on the west coast of Scotland as this was thought to be a better climate for Dennistoun's asthma. On each of these houses she spent enormous sums in alterations, lowering the staircase so that her invalid husband might negotiate the stairs more easily. Nothing improved the miserable Tiger so she purchased an estate in Hertfordshire called Temple Dinsley. By this time, he had two trained nurses in regular attendance. Yet another move took place to a house in the Isle of Wight and they finally ended up at the Red House, Hove. By the time Tiger died, Almina was flat broke having sold Seymour Place and all its contents. I was thoroughly disgusted.

Meanwhile the problem of estate duty still remained and I pored over the maps of the estate to decide which parcels of land should be sold or whether there were any other assets which could be turned into cash. I decided to go over our stock of silver to see which items might be surplus to requirements. When it came to considering Bingham, my estate in Nottinghamshire, I decided that it must go. It extended to twelve thousand acres and I was fortunate to sell it in one parcel through the good offices of Sir Trustram Eve.

Even then, having sold my best paintings, the pearls and silver, I still fell short of the total sum I had to find. Yet more land had to be sold and I had to part with the outlying and least attractive parts of the Highclere Estate. The sums I received, by present day standards, were pitifully small, but they all added to the total required by the Inland Revenue. At long last, after much anguish and many months of tedious negotiation, I was able to settle the account in full.

I then began to focus my attention on the bloodstock side, an area in which, after five years' intimate knowledge of horses, I felt I might have something to offer. Besides I had been an amateur rider and I found I had the knack of remembering individual horses, their owners, trainers and their performances on whichever racecourse they might have appeared. I had the help of Charlie Whincup who reigned supreme at the stud. A spare, lean countryman of medium height, he was too tall to be a jockey but had found his place in life as an excellent stud groom. A man of tradition, each Sunday he attended church wearing a grey bowler hat.

Charlie was delighted at my accession, for he knew of my intense interest in horses. Whereas my father had set up the stud and was keen on racing, his travels abroad prevented his direct personal involvement. As I explained to Charlie, I could see a good source of income in highly selective breeding. Thus I began a lifetime habit of daily visits to the stud to discuss the merits of our mares and the stallions to which we would send them. My career in bloodstock had begun.

14
On the Turf

As I became ever more involved in racing and breeding, I had the good fortune to meet, in 1928, Marcus Wickham-Boynton, who had been apprenticed to Atty Persse where he had learned the rudiments of becoming a trainer. Atty trained at Stockbridge and had the entrance to his stables through a large arch above which was the inscription: 'Ask no questions and you'll be told no lies.'

I asked Marcus if he would like to work for me as my stud manager. He agreed and we worked together, hunted together and went racing. He was a light-hearted, amusing companion and we had a lot of fun.

One day Marcus happened to mention that a two-year-old, belonging to Johnny Arkwright, trained by Atty Persse, should win at Kempton Park. The price was right, for when I went to Kempton I saw him marked up on the boards at sixteen to one. Summing up the rest of the runners, I decided that the colt looked a very good bet.

I went into the ring, took a thousand to sixty and then went back and had another look at the animal. He seemed very fit and right on his toes so I went back and took a thousand to eighty from Joe Baylis. Atty Persse had a commission agent named Charlie Mills. When Charlie heard what I had done, he executed a substantial commission for the stable. At the 'off' the starting price was nine to four and the horse duly won. The following morning I received a telegram from Atty: 'CONGRATULATIONS TO THE EARLY BIRD IN FUTURE HE IS UNLIKELY TO GET ANY WORMS.'

Later I discovered that it was through Charlie Mills that Atty had learned how Marcus and I had been instrumental in spoiling his market. Atty and I were tremendously fond of each other but our relationship cooled for a month or two. He thought we had taken unfair advantage of inside information as Marcus had been connected with Chattis Hill. However, he soon got over it and we remained the best of friends to the day of his death.

In those first early years of my marriage, soon after the war, life was a strange mixture of extremes. At one moment I would be fighting for the survival of my estates, at another I would be enjoying a luxurious week-end house party with the Marlboroughs.

My first visit to Blenheim had taken place when I was a very young man and the Ninth Duke of Marlborough had been my host. He was a pompous little man and I remember one Boxing Day, just as we were finishing breakfast and looking forward to a day's shooting, the butler came in and said, somewhat nervously, 'Your Grace, I have a message from your head keeper to say that he is ill and will not be able to come out shooting to-day. He wishes to assure Your Grace that he has delegated all his responsibilities to the keeper on the beat and he hopes you will have a good day.'

Sonny listened in chilly silence which communicated itself to all the guests.

'My compliments to my head keeper; will you please inform him that the lower orders are *never* ill.'

I was horrified at this reply but far too frightened to utter a word.

Gladys, the Duke's second wife (his first was Consuelo Vanderbilt), had a passion for King Charles spaniels and she housed about fifty of them in various bedrooms at the palace. They turned the place into a shambles and their smell pervaded the whole of the first floor. They had countless puppies and generally enjoyed a whale of a time.

The first occasion when I took Catherine to Blenheim was also at Christmas time and on this particular occasion Clemmie and Winston Churchill were among the guests.

We went downstairs for a drink before dinner to find Winston talking about the merits or demerits of various people as potential Prime Ministers. (He was at that time Chancellor of the Exchequer.) When there was a brief pause in his flow, I said I thought that had it not been for Edward Stanley's deafness he might well have made a very fine Prime Minister. Winston removed his cigar from his mouth and peered at me as if I were a worm.

'My dear Porchey,' he said, 'I can scarcely think of anybody who would make a *worse* Prime Minister.'

I was always somewhat frightened of him. Of course, he held the stage most of the time, recounting an endless stream of stories which I found enthralling. Whether he was lambasting Lloyd George or recalling the siege of Sidney Street or recounting his adventures during the Boer War, he exhilarated and delighted his audience. He hated interruptions and if, by chance, an ill-advised person had the temerity to interject a comment, he either totally ignored it or replied with such devastating scorn that the unfortunate individual would seldom speak again for the rest of the evening.

Even in those distant days, I saw Churchill as a man of undeniable stature, indeed of genius. He held me spellbound and nothing he achieved later surprised me at all. To me, at that time, he was already a giant among men.

That night at Blenheim, after a good dinner, with cigars well alight and glasses of brandy, Winston suddenly turned to me and said, 'There seems to be much controversy about my new betting tax. How do you think it's working, my dear Porchey?'

Treading a little warily, but feeling rather more secure on

a subject about which I knew something, I was able to answer him coherently for a change.

'Well, as you ask me, may I say that I think it's doing quite a lot of harm to racing and, in its present form, I fear it will bring you in very little money. I think there are different ways in which you might obtain revenue from racing.'

Winston's eyes lit up.

'My dear boy, if you can make me any suggestions I shall be delighted to have them.'

I was very pleased with the interest he showed and decided that after the Christmas holiday, I would waste no time in contacting Cardie Montagu to enlist his support in my endeavour to abolish the wretched betting tax of which I knew he equally disapproved

On Christmas Eve, we had our first day's shooting. That evening we attended that most heartwarming and traditional service in the religious calendar, midnight Mass, in the church which was packed with the tenants and people of Woodstock. Afterwards, as we walked out into the frosty air, the acrid smell of wood smoke pervaded our nostrils. Winston and I walked back to the palace together, and the world seemed to be so peaceful that it was difficult to reconcile the perils which he, Winston, was always warning us about.

Immediately upon return to Highclere, I telephoned Cardie and he suggested that we should enlist the help of Mr Joyce of Ladbrokes and our old friend, Arthur Bendir. As a quartet, we set about the problem of the betting tax and it took us six months to finish our proposals. In due course, I delivered it to Winston's official residence in Downing Street, beautifully typed and the folder bound with blue ribbon.

As anxious as an author delivering his first manuscript, I awaited the Great Man's reaction. After all, it had consumed our energies for nearly six months. It advocated various methods of betting with the main emphasis on the totalizator, save for allowing bookies to operate on the racecourses. They would merely act as agents for the tote in their offices. Thus, the country's vast expenditure on betting would be controlled by a central organization and the profits therefrom be reinvested in the industry, with increased prize money and innumerable other benefits, as well as producing revenue for the Chancellor of the Exchequer. But the weeks slipped by and we received no word from Winston.

It was at another house party, many months later, that I received the Chancellor's reaction.

'My dear Porchey,' he greeted me, 'I am most grateful for all the trouble you took in preparing your document. Evidently you put in a great deal of work but, in point of fact, I haven't read a word of it, because various of my officials seemed to share your view. We found that there was not much to be got out of this betting tax so I have decided to scrap it.'

My emotions on hearing this news were mixed. I felt he might at least have acknowledged the extent of our labours.

'I am very happy to hear it, Winston, and I hope that the next step will be for you to abolish all bookmakers except for those operating on the racecourses.'

'I shall never be a party to such a suggestion!' he roared. 'Why should I, a staunch upholder of democracy, deprive any man of earning an honest living. I might throw about half a million people out of work and I have no intention of doing so.'

I made no reply as he was obviously in no mood to brook any argument and I felt thoroughly disillusioned.

However I soon forgot all about the wayward workings of politics and shattered illusions for in 1924 Catherine produced my son and heir. We passed the happy news to all our friends and post-haste from Paris arrived not only the congratulations of the Vicomte de Fontarce but, as good as his word, his cheque for ten thousand pounds. This was a gesture I deeply appreciated; it is all too rare when a verbal commitment of yesteryear is honoured to the letter.

We christened our son Henry in the Church of St Michael

and All Angels just outside the park. Prince George, Duke of Kent, son of George V, very kindly agreed to be one of the godfathers. He was a great friend of the family, very fond of my wife and a frequent visitor to Highclere. Of one thing I was determined: my son, and my daughter Penelope, who was to follow him, would never lack love and affection. There would be no repetition of the wretched and outmoded parent–child relationship that had existed in my youth.

Slowly life at Highclere, although modest by comparison with the past, was beginning to assume normality again. Now that some of my financial pressures had decreased, I felt able to gratify my great interest in shooting and decided to form a syndicate of four paying guns. Cocky Dundonald, Murray Graham, Cardie Montagu and Joe Whitburn each paid fifteen hundred pounds.

For the next three years our syndicate flourished magnificently and everyone thoroughly enjoyed themselves. It came to an end in the following manner. One day Cardie said to me, 'Shooting at Highclere, I imagine, is like shooting high pheasants in heaven. We have had the greatest possible fun and we all think the time has come to end on such a happy note.'

I felt that he was quite right and in some ways I was rather relieved that my responsibilities in this matter had come to an end. For I was spending more and more of my time studying horses, working out form and generally steeping myself in racing. I also hoped to cover my expenses by putting my knowledge to good use. During the years covered by this story I won twenty-eight thousand pounds betting. When you think of the turnover of capital involved, this has always seemed to me a miserly reward for the time and trouble taken.

Jock Broughton, or to give him his full title, Sir Delves Broughton, lived at Doddington Hall, Nantwich, Cheshire. His wife, Vera, was a lovely woman who bore an amazing resemblance to Gladys Cooper. Jock used to keep a few moderate horses, trained by Ronald Farquharson, two of which were very successful, two geldings called Prospero and Highwayside.

Whenever he had had a bad week betting, he used to bring out one of these old horses, pop it into a selling plate, have about a thousand pounds on it, usually at a very short price, and it nearly always won. Usually there was no bid made for his winner so he bought it in, ready for next time.

Vera was marvellous company and I frequently stayed with them at Doddington and went hunting with the local hounds. One day I suggested to Vera that we should go to Newmarket. We had a very enjoyable afternoon and, while Vera was talking to some acquaintances, up came another good friend of mine, Billy Bass, who was acting as a steward.

He sniffed, twiddled his moustaches and said, 'Look here, Porchey, you know quite well you've no business to bring an actress into the private stand.'

'My dear Billy, I have *not* brought any actress into the stands, I can assure you.'

'Oh, yes you have. Everyone knows it; we've all been watching you with Gladys Cooper.'

'I beg your pardon, Billy. I have not brought Gladys Cooper here. I know the rules perfectly well.'

Then I told him who she was and he immediately said he would like to be introduced to her as he thought she was so lovely. Rock Cholmondoley also asked for an introduction. I made the same reply that Mrs Patrick Campbell used nightly in *Pygmalion*, 'Not bloody likely!'

Jock Broughton indirectly again landed me in trouble on another occasion. It was after much discussion and heart-searching that I decided that my most hopeful breeding prospect was a little mare by Charles O'Malley out of Wild Arum named Malva. She had won the Champagne Stakes at Salisbury and a handicap at Bath. She was first mated with my father's stallion, Franklin, who had been second in the St Leger in 1921 and produced a little filly called Frankly which won a thousand-pound race at Birmingham. I then decided to send Malva to Dick Dawson's stallion Blandford, at a fee of four hundred guineas which, in that day, was a not inconsiderable sum. (This was, if you remember, the stallion I had tried to buy when I was in Constantinople.) The result of that match was a colt to whom I gave the name Blenheim. I decided he must be sold as a yearling and I put him into Tattersall's July sale, without reserve.

The weekend before Blenheim was due to come up for sale, Catherine's younger brother was staying with us at Highclere. Tragically, after dinner, he suffered a stroke and never regained consciousness. It was Catherine's wish that he should be buried at Highclere.

Realizing that I would be unable to attend the sale, I decided to ring up Jock Broughton and explain the situation. I told him I was running two animals at the meeting, one a filly called Doushka, by Tetratema out of Dorval, in the Girton Handicap, ridden by Charlie Smirke, and, as I thought she would win, asked him to put me £200 on her. Also on the Wednesday, I was running a mare called Mara, by Alan Breck out of Maranon, in the Falmouth Stakes and, as I thought she was also likely to win, asked him to put a monkey on her.

When he agreed to carry out these commissions, I said, 'Hold on, Jock, I've got another problem. Also on Wednesday, my yearlings are coming up for sale. One of them is a very nice colt by Dick Dawson's stallion Blandford. His name is Blenheim. I've got a hunch that Dick wants to buy him for the Aga which will probably mean that George Lambton will be bidding. I like the colt very much and I'm determined that he should make four thousand pounds. I would be most grateful if you would bid up to that.

'Of course I will,' said Jock, 'hope your two animals oblige. I'll telephone you on Wednesday evening.'

Everything went according to plan. Both my horses won and Blenheim was knocked down for four thousand two hundred guineas to George Lambton on behalf of the Aga Khan.

We buried my brother-in-law in the cemetery at Highclere in a grave lined with moss into which thousands of water lilies were placed.

I had given no further thought to my recent sale when I went to the second July meeting at Newmarket. Having ridden work in the morning, I had a good breakfast in the Jockey Club rooms, after which, with my pipe firmly clenched between my teeth, I walked up towards the sale paddocks. It was a glorious morning. Suddenly, a loud voice cut across my thoughts.

'Porchey!' and again, 'P-O-R-C-H-E-Y! I want a word with you.'

The very timbre of the voice spelt trouble. I stopped in my tracks and turned round to find Gerald Deane, whom I knew quite well, storming up behind me. Late of the 11th Hussars, he was a partner in Tattersalls, as indeed his son is to-day. He was a man of uncertain temper and could be very aggressive.

'Good morning, Gerald,' I said quietly, 'what on earth's the matter?'

'What's the matter, you ask me? I'll tell you what's the matter! Of all the stupid things you have ever done, you did one of the most stupid the other day.'

Completely mystified, I asked him what he was so cross about.

'You know perfectly well that for some reason, when you didn't come to the last sale, you put in Jock Broughton to bid up that colt of yours, Blenheim, when it was clearly advertised that the horse was to be sold without reserve. You *know* this is against our rules. What's more, I'm telling you here and now that if you ever try any tricks like that again, Tattersalls will never accept another entry from you for the rest of your life.'

For a moment I paused.

'All right, Gerald ...' I said quietly, trying to calm him.

'And don't try to deny it,' Deane said aggressively, 'everyone knows perfectly well that Jock Broughton has never paid anything more than a monkey for any animal he's ever bought in his life. The moment I saw him bidding three and a half thousand, four thousand pounds, I knew what was going on.'

I remained impassive, standing quietly, for everything the man had said was perfectly true; besides which, I didn't want to anger him any further by trying to give him the explanation.

'Anyway, Porchey, you've had your warning. Don't let it ever happen again.'

There was to be a sequel. The colt was entered for the Derby and, being a very old friend of the Aga's, I stood beside him watching the race. He had two horses running, Blenheim and Rustom Pasha, the latter being the Aga's fancy and, by a strange coincidence, I drew this horse in the Derby Club sweep. I sold him for two hundred and twenty pounds and reinvested two hundred on Blenheim at 25-1. He was ridden by Harry Wragg.

They were a hundred and fifty yards from home when Wragg shot Blenheim into the lead and, with my heart thumping with excitement, I cheered Blenheim home. But the Aga, who was very short-sighted, could only see his colours in the lead and started shouting at the top of his voice.

'Rustom wins, Rustom wins.'

'No, he doesn't, you bloody fool. *Blenheim* wins.'

It mattered little to the Aga, for he owned both horses.

'Never mind,' he said, 'Rustom will win the Eclipse.' And so he did.

We ran forward to meet the triumphant horse and jockey. The Aga was handed the reins and together we walked toward the winner's enclosure. As we did so, a thought leapt into my mind.

'Now, one thing, my dear Aga, before you forget about this great achievement. As I bred this horse, I hope that you will give me a free nomination for every year that he stands at stud?'

There was only a fraction of a pause from one of the richest men in the world, but one who was known to be extremely tight-fisted. Then, 'Certainly not; you will pay the same as anyone else.'

We were the greatest of friends and he frequently stayed with us at Highclere. One thing could be said about the Aga – his word was truly his bond. But he was by no means a charitable institution; indeed the reverse and, upon occasion, could be less than generous. But we knew each other so well that, with the tumultuous cheers of the crowd ringing in our ears, the spirit of the occasion brooked no sense of hurt. I was thrilled and wildly excited at having had the luck to breed a Derby winner, even if I no longer owned him.

Many years later, after Jock Broughton and Vera were divorced, he married again and lived in Kenya. One day Lord Errol, a friend and neighbour, was found shot dead. Jock Broughton was suspected and charged with his murder. Personally, I never had any doubt that he did not do it. So far as fighting situations were concerned, Jock was a timid man, had a broken wrist and was a very poor shot. In due course he was tried and acquitted. I immediately sent him the following cable: 'HEARTY CONGRATULATIONS UNDERSTAND YOU WON A NECK CLEVERLY REGARDS PORCHEY.'

Jimmy de Rothschild was so amused when he heard about the cable that he arranged for it to be framed and hung in the bar at White's.

Sad to relate, poor old Jock returned to England and committed suicide at a hotel in Liverpool. He had little money left and had sold various goods and chattels belonging to his family who were far from pleased.

Some of my very close friends, like Jock, were owners, but others were, like myself, occasional amateur riders. One such was Harry Atherton Brown. Educated at Eton, he was a very good shot, an excellent rider, particularly good over fences, but also more than adequate on the flat.

Harry never had much money but he was a great gambler and loved betting. He trained his own horses and also trained horses for his great friend, Hugo Londesborough and for the occasional American owner introduced to him by me. The girls were usually head over heels in love with Harry, for he was debonair and very sexy.

The year that his horse The Bore ran in the Grand National, I went up and stayed with Eddy Derby at Knowsley. Harry was riding The Bore and had backed himself to win £10,000 at four to one from bookmakers who laid him these bets against him getting round. He also backed his horse each way at ten to one and had a single place bet of £15,000–£5,000 laid to him by Issy Isaacs.

I had had a good bet on Trespasser in the Imperial Cup and, as I was watching the horse being unsaddled, I saw George Poole standing by the weighing room with his cigarette hanging from the corner of his lips.

'Hello, George. What do you know?'

'Well, I know something that'll interest you,' he replied. 'You backed the last winner, didn't you?'

'I sure did,' I said.

'Then go and have £100 on Shaun Spadah for the National. I train him for McAlpine and I can only tell you this, he's never been better. Dick Rees rode him this morning and, my word, I think with a little luck at the price – twenty to one – you should get a damned good run.'

I walked across and did exactly as suggested. Then I had £50 each way The Bore at ten to one and finally had four fifties on The Bore getting round.

The race began like so many Nationals before and after; a field of hopefuls and many fallers. With the Liverpool crowd roaring their encouragement, only two horses came up to the second last fence; unbelievably, they were Shaun Spadah and The Bore. Shaun Spadah was leading The Bore and he jumped it perfectly when, to my horror, what did I see? Harry crashed with poor old Bore, shot over the fence but not in company with his horse. Miraculously, he managed to retain a grip on one broken rein. As he got up, I saw him put his right hand up to his left shoulder while still clutching the rein. Somewhat jerkily, he tottered round the fence, confused and in pain, to where the horse stood waiting. A couple of willing spectators helped Harry remount. With his left arm hanging limp, he turned the horse back forty or fifty yards, swung him round, and, kicking old Bore, pointed him at the fence. I could hardly believe my eyes.

The crowd cheered and the horse, sensing their encouragement, quickened from a trot to a canter and somehow, by the mercy of God, they managed to clear it. I feel sure the acclamation of the racegoers could have been heard in Ireland as disabled rider and horse struggled up to the winning post. It was nothing less than heroic of both horse and man.

Happily, it turned out that Harry had only broken his collar bone, not his arm. However, there was to be a last minute panic. Pale, and in great pain, Harry was unable to carry his saddle into the weighing room. He sat on the scales, only to find that he couldn't quite draw the weight. Suddenly, someone remembered the bridle. The rules of racing allowed that, on failing to draw the weight, the horse's bridle could be added. Harry's bridle was removed from his horse and he just drew the right weight. My three wagers on the National won me two thousand, eight hundred and twenty-five pounds.

Catherine and I often held house-parties at Highclere on week-ends when nearby racecourses were holding meetings. Newbury was our nearest racecourse, but we were within easy reach of Windsor and Ascot. Among frequent guests on these occasions were Arthur Portman and his wife.

Arthur Portman was the proprietor of *Horse and Hound* and also its editor. A most curious man, a *bon viveur*, loving good food and good wine, smoking the best cigars, he was also a clever punter, never betting on a handicap, only on weight for age races and that is a very good tip for anyone. Where he excelled among all the racing men I have ever known, was in his ability to sift all the statistical information he could obtain in order to provide the logical answer. He took immense trouble with the form book and got all the dope he could from the trainers themselves. If two equally fancied horses were in the same race, he would first study their form, then tout the two trainers. Having considered their remarks, he would make his decision. He was usually right.

Another great friend was Buck Barclay. He was an exceptionally good-looking man, tall and upright, who in his heyday had been a marvellous rider to hounds, a good amateur over fences, one of the greatest salmon fishermen of his day and a very fine shot. He told me that of all the experiences in a long and colourful life, there was nothing to rival the thrill of the first run of a salmon: 'If you were to ask me what has been my greatest fun, I would tell you, without hesitation, that it's salmon fishing.' Because of his fine reputation, the Jockey Club had appointed him a judge. In those days, judges had nothing to guide them except their eyesight and on one memorable occasion at Windsor, he *unhesitatingly* gave a verdict of a triple dead-heat. As it happened, at the self-same moment, a spectator took a photograph and proved his decision correct.

As well as such old friends as Portman and Barclay I often encountered an old acquaintance of my father's at race meetings called Tom King. Although never a member of the Jockey Club, Tom was a member of the National Hunt Committee and dearly beloved by all. When he was admitted to hospital with incurable cancer, I used to visit him three or four times each week and one evening I told him that I was going to Ascot and would call in the next day to tell him the results.

I was walking through the paddock when I was approached by another good friend whose nickname to one and all was Boozy Boo. It was Sir Robert Buchanan-Jardine. He was a 'bottle-of-whisky-a-day' man and one of the kindest and most generous I have ever known.

'Hello, Porchey,' he called, 'wanted to have a word with you. It's about our old friend Tom. Is there any better news?'

'No, alas. I'm afraid it won't be long now.'

At this, he began to poke around in a capacious waistcoat pocket and brought forth a folded piece of paper which turned out to be a cheque, which had already been made out.

'This is a little something for Tom. Would you give it to him when next you see him and say it is an affectionate greeting in the hope that he'll soon feel better. Tell him it's in memory of the many happy outings we have spent together and I hope there will be many more.'

Suddenly I felt a lump in my throat.

'I can't tell you what this will mean to Tom,' I said, 'you see, I happen to know that he is worried about money, especially one or two debts which, because of his illness, he has been unable to repay. This will make all the difference and I shall give it to him this evening.'

After the last race was over, I hurried to the hospital.

'Hello, Tom, how are you? I've seen an old friend of yours who sends his affectionate greetings.'

'Who was that?' he enquired.

'Old Boo, and he asked me to give you this little gift.'

It was a cheque for £5,000. For a moment he was stunned and then tears began to well into his eyes.

'Oh, how can I thank him ... oh Porchey, what a godsend. Please thank him for me because now I shall be able to clear off all my debts and die happy.'

During a visit to South Africa in 1925 I had a great stroke of luck which enabled me to pay for the whole trip, the fares and all the travel within South Africa for Catherine and myself as well. But my success did not come from backing a horse, nor did anyone give me a blank cheque; it came about in the following way.

Catherine and I, in company with Sir Hedworth and Lady Meux were guests of Abe Bailey in Cape Town at Ruist-en-Vrede, which in English means 'Rest in Peace', and we all enjoyed his splendid hospitality. After about a week in Cape Town, Catherine and I, Harry Cottrill and his wife, plus Sidney Beer, went off to stay for a fortnight at Abe's farm at Colesberg where we rode daily and generally had a peaceful time until Abe started making passes at Catherine, though she was able to fend him off most adroitly. Harry and Jessie Cottrill were with us because Abe trained a few horses with Harry – his principal trainer at the time being the greatly respected and charming Reggie Day, of whom Abe used to say, 'Every dog has his day and I have got Reggie Day.'

On our way home, we spent a few days at the Carlton Hotel in Johannesburg where a most amusing incident took place. Abe's *homme d'affaires* was Sir Julius Jeppe and he phoned me one day and said his boss had suggested I might like to see the 'call over' at the Stock Exchange. I told him that I would be delighted to do so and so he picked me up and drove me there to witness the proceedings. Whilst sitting in the visitors' gallery before the day's business began, Jeppe told me that Abe had suggested that I should buy five thousand East Rands which he felt sure would go up five or six shillings in the very near future. Knowing Abe's reputation, I was most intrigued. Very little business appeared to be done until East Rand flashed up on the Board when all hell broke loose and all the Brokers present appeared to wish to sell East Rands which had opened at around thirty-five shillings.

At this stage I excused myself for a few moments, ostensibly to go to the loo. Jeppe handed me the key to his private lavatory and called the commissionaire to show me where it was. As soon as I was safely out of Jeppe's sight, I asked the commissionaire where the nearest cable office was situated and he replied that it was in Union Street, just across the road. I ran across and sent the following full-rate cable to my brokers in London: 'SELL FIVE THOUSAND EAST RANDS AT BEST THE MOMENT DEALINGS COMMENCE SIGNED CARNARVON.' When I sent this cable, it was 8.30 a.m. in London. That evening, I received a return cable from Keith, Bayley and Rigg: 'SOLD FIVE THOUSAND EAST RANDS AT THIRTY THREE AND SIXPENCE AT CLOSE ALL SELLERS

AROUND TWENTY SEVEN SHILLINGS.' Happily, I paid for my trip to South Africa, making about two and a half thousand profit, but not quite in the way Abe had expected.

While in South Africa, I attended a dinner at the Rand Club in Johannesburg. The occasion was in honour of Sir Abe Bailey who was a contemporary of Cecil Rhodes.

Only men were present and when the meal had ended and the time for speeches had come, one of Abe's friends rose to propose his health. To the great amusement of all the leviathans present, he began by saying, 'Gentlemen, we are here tonight to do honour to that great patriot, Sir Abe Bailey, whom we all know has been one of the founders of the prosperity in the Union. I think I can best pay tribute to his achievements by paraphrasing the words which are carved on Cecil Rhodes' tomb, "So little done, so much to do." On this occasion, I hope you will all agree that I may say of him, "So many done, so few to do."'

Back in England after our South African trip we continued with our week-end parties. In the evenings after dinner we would sit by the fire, drink and tell each other good stories. One evening George Lambton, a remarkably handsome man who had an enormous success with beautiful ladies throughout his life, told me of an amusing incident that had occurred at Highclere many years before.

He was having an affair at the time with a lady who, with her husband, was staying with my father. Her husband was a good deal older than she, myopic and rather a bore. When she arrived at Highclere and found George, she was enraptured.

'Oh, darling, how exciting, how wonderful. I can't wait to take you in my arms again.'

'Neither can I,' agreed George, 'but I don't see how we can manage it this week-end.'

'Oh, yes we can,' his girl friend declared, 'let me show you the north library. At night-time they only light one or two lamps and it's always very dark; sometimes no lamps are lit at all. After dinner, I'll make an excuse and get away from the ladies. You find a reason to leave the dining room and I'll wait for you in there. You'll find me in one of those marvellous big chairs.'

George was more than delighted and the assignation took place exactly as planned. As he opened the door, he received a whispered greeting.

'Over here, darling,' and shortly he was happily making love. Seconds later they were both taken very much by surprise as the library door opened and someone came in. Walking straight to the bookcase, a short-sighted man climbed up the little pair of steps and began to gaze along the rows of books, seeking one that he intended to read.

'It's my husband!' she whispered into George's ear, 'Ssh, ssh, you slip out and get behind the chair; then I'll get him out of the room. George did exactly as bidden and she tiptoed out of the room, turning the handle noisily as she re-entered.

'Hello darling,' she said, 'I wondered where you were. What on earth are you doing?'

'Just looking for a book, my dear. It's so damned dark in here, I've had a hell of a job finding it. I've got it now though.'

'Good,' she exlaimed, 'now we'd better go back and rejoin the others.'

The anecdotes we told each other did not always involve racing, love or money, many were concerned with shooting or hunting. Harry Dalmeny, later to become Lord Rosebery, was a great friend of mine and I've never known anyone more full of charm. He used to say, 'I'm not half a Jew and half a Scotsman for nothing.'

Dalmeny had a great sense of humour and a brilliant intellect. I was present on that great occasion which has now become famous when, out hunting with the Whaddon Chase of which he was the Master at the time, he went up to Nubar Gulbenkian and said, 'I've never seen anybody wearing an orchid in his pink coat before,' to which Nubar replied, 'I am quite sure you are correct, Master, but I wonder if you have ever seen an Armenian out hunting before.'

On the very same afternoon we saw a further side to Harry's many faceted character. There was another follower of the hunt who was known to be something of a bounder. Lady Derby was just manœuvering her horse as we were at one of those bullfinches where you have to take your turn, when the man shouted, 'Go on old lady, get on with it, you're holding us up!' Lady Derby replied coldly, 'Yes, I am old; I'm certainly a lady. Jump if you wish, I shall follow at my leisure.'

Some ten minutes later the incident was brought to the notice of the Master, whereupon Harry called the man over: 'I understand you have been exceedingly rude to Lady Derby. You will go home immediately and never come out again. If you don't make off this instant, I shall take hounds home.'

On another occasion, going to a meet in the village of Wing, Harry and I dismounted to relieve ourselves. Gibbs, his second horseman called out, 'Excuse me m'Lord, Lady Derby's just trotting up.'

Without batting an eyelid, the Master replied, 'My dear Gibbs, there are only two sorts of women in this world; those that have seen and those that want to see, and Lady Alice is not in the latter category.'

Harry had a divine step-daughter, Lavinia, who when she grew up married Bernard Norfolk. She was very young when I first knew her and I well remember her riding a pony called Tango. She loved horses and I occasionally gave her a mount on one of my hunters. Her mother, Eva Belper, was also a great rider to hounds and she and Harry made a great success of their marriage and she bore him a son to inherit his father's title.

I too enjoyed hunting and one winter in those carefree inter-war years, I took Lowesby Hall in Leicestershire from Bert Marlborough as he had decided to go on a safari in Africa. I had half-a-dozen nice hunters up there and enjoyed many days with the Quorn and the Belvoir.

One day, whilst out hunting with the Belvoir, hounds

were running on a breast-high scent, my friend Monica Sheriffe was quite close to me, dear old Brose Clark was a bit to our left and Mrs Pilkington on my right. We were advancing towards the Smite which is rather a broad stream, and one had to put on quite a bit of pace to jump it. Brose Clark's horse refused and we heard him say, 'Okay, horse, that looks like the Hudson River to me.'

Meanwhile, Monica had shouted to Mrs Pilkington to 'mind that tree' – she was riding a chestnut horse which, I think, was somewhat out of control. Monica and I landed safely on the other side but Mrs Pilkington had caught a branch of the tree and was flat on her back. We stopped and dismounted and Monica held my horse. When I picked Mrs Pilkington up, I saw that the whole of the top half of her nose had been sliced off as if with a carving knife. Mercifully she had been knocked out, so I put my coat under her head and, whilst doing so, noticed the missing bit of her nose had fallen on top of a tuft of grass. I picked it up, stuck it on again – it was quite clean – tied my bandana handkerchief tight around it and asked Monica to gallop off to a nearby farmhouse and get help. Mrs Pilkington was then taken to hospital in Melton and when her nose was stitched on again the traces were hardly visible. Afterwards her dear mother wrote me the sweetest of letters returning my bandana handkerchief freshly washed and ironed.

While on the subject of Monica Sheriffe, I must relate a little tale about darling Mon which gave me great pleasure at the time and, in retrospect, she can only feel very flattered if she remembers the occasion. We were dining together at the Embassy Club and Luigi had put us at a table just on the left of the door which was always occupied by the Prince of Wales whenever he went there. Halfway through our meal, the Aga Khan, who was dining with a large party facing us on the other side of the room, wrote a note to me and sent it across by the head waiter. It read as follows: 'As usual, you have a really lovely girl dining with you. With that blue-black hair and glorious complexion, I feel she cannot be anything but *une belle Circassienne*. I am coming over to be introduced. Yours ever, A.K.'

Whilst I was staying at the Station Hotel in Nottingham with some friends for a couple of days' shooting at Bingham, I invited the Reverend Hutt to shoot with me. He rode a cob, wore a black Billy Cock hat which was similar to a bowler, and was, in every sense of the word, an old-fashioned country parson.

One day, when we were shooting together, one of the beaters who was known as Wingy (because he had only one arm) came over to me after the drive.

'Excuse me, m'Lord, you shot me.'

I saw some blood running down his cheek.

'I'm most awfully sorry,' I said, 'how the hell did I do that?'

'That there partridge you shot stone dead – one pellet ricochetted off his leg and got me. It wasn't your fault.'

I pulled out a five pound note and handed it to him.

'Thank you very much, m'Lord, you're a real gentleman.'

The Reverend Hutt who had been standing next to me said, 'My dear Lord Carnarvon, you mustn't do that again. Wingy is a real rascal and has been quite successful in earning himself a bit extra by his little trick. He carries a little bottle of blood and, at an opportune moment, dabs it on his face.' He continued, 'Now, I'm afraid I shall have to ask you to forgive me for not lunching with you to-day – I have a funeral to conduct – but when I have finished, I'll join you at the pub and have a pint of beer and a bit of Stilton. That's all I shall need before we resume shooting.'

I used to enjoy immensely riding in Bumper's races. For fourteen years I rode work at Whatcombe, where my horses were trained at the time. I kept very fit and I had quite a lot of success with the limited opportunities that there were in those days for amateur riders.

Once I rode in a race at Salisbury called the Wallop Selling Plate of two hundred sovereigns when there were only five runners. I rode a horse of my own called Straight Flush, which I had bought for only fifty guineas as a yearling because he was so straight in front. George Duller, perhaps the best jockey I have ever seen over hurdles and extremely good on the rare occasions he rode on the flat, was riding a horse of his father's called Saintly Sinner, in the same race. My horse, incredibly, was favourite and on the way down to the post, George said to me, 'This old horse of my father's was in a field about a week ago, so he wants you to win. He hopes to get a bit of surplus and then all will be well.'

After we had gone about six furlongs in this mile race, George raced alongside and shouted at me, 'Go on, hit him.'

I attempted to do so and George replied, 'You only tickled him, give him another or I shall have to say goodbye.'

I was convulsed with laughter and George went on and won. There was no bid for the winner, but George never stopped pulling my leg for many years afterwards. He was a charming man and his widow, Bessie, who subsequently married Walter Nightingall, has always remained one of my many good friends.

Whilst on the subject of that famous race, the Wallop Selling Plate, I rode a horse in it called Centaur on 7 July 1932, which I had given my wife as a yearling. This race was won by Alec Cottrill on Anthurium who beat Ginger Wellesley on Roi des Enfers with Mr J. Corbett third on Mittagong. I came in fourth on Centaur who was an awful dog and never tried a yard but Dick Dawson who had found him very useful as a lead horse, had thought he might get a place.

Despite my final position, this was the most fascinating race in which I have ever taken part. Mittagong was a hot favourite and probably should have won. Ginger Wellesley, a very good amateur, lost his temper with Corbett and started hitting both Corbett and his horse about a furlong from home. The latter responded by belabouring Ginger and his mount. This they did up to the winning post, much to the amusement of the crowd who had never seen such a sight.

I was called in by the stewards a few minutes after the race. The stewards acting were Billy Bass, Joe Whitburn and

Humphrey de Trafford. Billy said, 'Please tell us what you saw of this disgraceful behaviour.'

Not wishing to get Ginger into trouble, I told him that I was so busy riding my own horse that I had seen nothing.

For a moment there was silence, then Billy retorted, 'You are as great a liar as most jockeys whenever I ask them anything of this description. Get out.'

The stewards immediately disqualified these two horses and so Centaur was placed second, much to the delight of Dick Dawson. Anthurium, the winner, was then bought for three hundred guineas by Prince Aly Khan, a great friend of mine as was his father, the Aga Khan.

Shortly after this, I received a letter from Gavin Hamilton, who was Ginger Wellesley's godfather, thanking me profusely for what he described as 'your very chivalrous behaviour which, I am sure, saved my godson from being warned off the turf'.

I did a lot of betting at different times for the Aga and perhaps one of the most extraordinary happenings occurred when he ran a horse in the Leger called Salmon Trout. Both Dick Dawson and I, indeed all concerned, were extremely confident of this horse winning, as we had taken him over to Stockbridge and galloped him with a horse called Twelve Pointer and one or two others of Atty's good animals and Salmon Trout had won the gallop very convincingly. The Aga instructed me to put £1,000 on his horse for him and I had £500 myself. I asked Jack Clayton to do this commission for me as he was a very big punter and Arthur Bendir would always lay him a big bet, whereas I would have been unlikely to get much on, particularly as I was intimately connected with the stable. Jack returned me five to one to the money and at the time I was quite satisfied. Carslake was retained by the Aga that year but Brownie thought that it was a good thing for Polyphontes – owned by another old friend of mine, Solly Joel.

Carslake went to a bookmaker called Mo Tarsh and suggested to him that he should lay him the odds to £1,000

Polyphontes. Tarsh replied that he would do so providing Carslake would lay him seven thousand to one thousand against Salmon Trout. Carslake agreed to do this.

Rumours of this Machiavellian plot became known and Salmon Trout went out steadily in the betting to ten to one on the day of the race. I received a message from the Aga to tell Carslake that he would get half of the entire stake, instead of the usual ten per cent, if he won. I delivered this message to Carslake and I told him in the weighing room, before he went out to mount, that we were well aware of his fancy for the favourite. Nevertheless, we considered Salmon Trout was a racing certainty and he had better remember my words.

To cut a long story short, not until Carslake saw that a horse of Barclay Walker's called Santorb had definitely beaten Polyphontes did he make any effort to win. He then set Salmon Trout alight and in the last hundred yards won, going away by about two lengths. He was a great jockey but a real villain.

Immediately after the race, he asked me when he could have the money promised by the Aga. I told him he would get the whole amount – somewhere in the region of £6,000 – in about a fortnight. He said he'd like it immediately. I told him that was quite impossible.

Half an hour before the race I took £2,000 to £200 from Harry Slowburn, and Charlie Mills – who heard me do so – told me that Issy Isaacs, a first cousin of Sir Rufus Isaacs, both having been brought up together in the Mile End Road, would be delighted to lay me ten to one to £300 if I would like to have it, so I took that as well and in the end won £7,500.

Sometimes my luck held good. There was a lugubrious character who loved hunting and had earned the nickname 'jump for joy and fall for fun'. He owned a racehorse called Black Gown which was to run in a three-horse, five-furlong, weight-for-age race at Newmarket. The hot favourite was a horse owned by Lord Astor at odds on. I had no intention of betting, but the moment I saw the favourite coming toward the paddock, I detected that he was walking lame. I looked again, wondering if I had made a mistake. 'This horse won't run,' I thought to myself, 'and if he does run, he certainly won't win.' I dashed down to the rails to find that Black Gown was being freely offered at six and seven to one. I asked no questions, thinking that, in the absence of the hot favourite, Black Gown would probably win and so I had seven hundred to one with Ted Rowson of Cooper and Rowson, then I walked a little bit further down the rails and said to dear old Joe Baylis, 'I'm going to take a chance and have seven hundred to one Black Gown, if that's agreeable to you.'

'Oh,' he said, 'that's agreeable enough and what's more, I'd give anything to see the Major win.'

Deciding that fourteen hundred to two was quite sufficient, I walked away to see if the favourite would indeed run. Sure enough, at the very last moment he was withdrawn, and Black Gown did all that I had expected of him. By doing no more than studying the runners before the race, I had won £1,400.

Backing my own hunches and carrying out commissons for others did not always end in success. Indeed one of my forays for Jimmy de Rothschild was disastrous.

At the time I was staying with him at his magnificent house at Waddesdon which now belongs to the National Trust. The interior of this building was brought from France and mounted within the outer walls. In some rooms, solid pink and white marble extends from the floor to the ceiling, requiring no decoration and giving the room a warmth and glow that might be thought impossible from the use of natural stone.

Jimmy suffered the misfortune of losing an eye from a misdirected golf ball but it in no way impaired his love of beauty nor, indeed, his keen interest in racing. His colours were blue and yellow and with his sallow complexion earned him the nickname the Yellow Peril, chiefly because at times he really shook the ring with a lucky coup.

On this occasion he had a horse running at Epsom called Snow Leopard which he thought had a good chance of winning. Jimmy asked me, Cardy Montagu, William Rawle and Fred Cripps to do his commission. He wanted £12,000 on his horse, so I was instructed to do my best in Tattersalls and invest £3,000 for him. The other three were to line up near the rails and when Cardy removed his hat, they were to start operations simultaneously and get on £3,000 each. On this occasion, any lesser man would have turned ashen: Snow Leopard was beaten by a short head and the average of the commission had worked out at about four to one to the money. After the race was over, I told Jimmy how sorry I was that the coup had failed and all he said was, 'My dear friend, I shall now rename him Slow Leopard.'

Epsom was one of my favourite courses. For many years fifty of us formed a club and took over the Lonsdale Stand calling it the Booth. Hugh Lonsdale presided and always saw to it that glorious lunches were provided. As a rule, at the spring meeting, there would be scores of plovers' eggs, masses of caviare, cold lobsters and a wonderful collection of wines. At the Derby, he used to supply huge bowls of wild strawberries which were the *piece de résistance*. I still reflect on the glorious fun that I had in the Booth and wish it could have continued for longer than it did.

Hugh was a great trencherman who used to eat gargantuan breakfasts when at home. His first course was usually a dish of damsons which he ate walking round the dining room. This was followed by the most enormous helpings of either egg and bacon or kidneys and bacon, kedgeree, or something of that order. He would then cut himself several slices of cold ham and this would be washed down with copious draughts of Hock. He would then top up, if one can believe it and I promise you it is true, with a large glass of liqueur brandy. Such was his modest breakfast. After this he would light one of his monumental cigars, supplied to him in various sizes to match different occasions, which were made of a tobacco specially chosen for its mildness. Personally, I thought they tasted like chopped hay and would never smoke them.

Hugh had a never-ending fund of tall stories, frequently based on fact but with the dividing line between truth and fiction finely drawn. It always amused me to hear him say to his wife, after telling some very tall tale, 'Isn't that so, Gracie?' and to hear her reply, 'I have often heard you say so, Hugh.'

He was a man who had a great, and in some ways unique, affinity with animals. He could teach his dogs all sorts of tricks and his own pony, upon which he rode when out grouse-shooting, was so obedient that when he got to his butt, he would tell it to lie down until the drive was over. It was quite extraordinary: the aimal seemed to know exactly what he had said and immediately complied.

One of the stories Hugh loved to tell was of an occasion when he was out hunting with the Duke of Beaufort's hounds. Apparently, he was up with hounds but with neither huntsman nor whips in sight. The fox, hard pressed, leapt into a canal and, quickly followed by his pursuers, scrambled out on the other side. The Yellow Earl came to a sudden halt, his determination to be in at the death temporarily thwarted. Happily, he saw a slow moving horse-drawn barge coming into view. Trotting along the bank to meet it, he sought permisson to land on the stern of the barge and then leap off on to the bank on the other side. The old bargee, somewhat astounded, laughed and gave his assent. Turning to his horse, the Earl cantered a little way into the field, spoke to the horse and patted it, then urged it forward. With one tremendous leap they struck the flat stern, took off instantly and landed safely on the other side. Normally, I would have pigeon-holed this as a very tall story but, knowing his ability with animals, it might just possibly have been true.

Hugh Lonsdale spent money like water and when he drove out from Lowther in his yellow carriage, adorned with a yellow waistcoat with two enormous pockets full of silver coins, he would scatter these to the children on the estate whenever they opened a gate. He loved to hear their cries of 'good old Lonny' ringing in his ears.

When I was staying at Lowther one August, many of the usual guests were there, Billy and Noreen Bass, the Mar and Kellys, Prince Arthur of Connaught and an American lady who had never been before. Dinner was announced and Hugh put this lady on his right. After we had finished the soup, the American asked Hugh if she might smoke, to which he replied, 'My dear lady, I don't mind if you burn. I shall order the coffee immediately.'

I have never seen a woman so completely crushed. I don't think she uttered another word during the entire evening.

Catherine and I very nearly did burn on one occasion. We were staying at the National Stud, which at that time was located in Ireland. It had been donated to the nation by Willie Hall Walker, later Lord Wavertree, and we were house guests of its first director, Harry Greer.

It was in the middle of the night that the shouted warnings of 'fire' aroused us from our slumbers. It was obvious that we needed to evacuate pretty damned quickly. I threw a gown to Catherine, and sweeping up her jewellery, we successfully located the stairs and hurried out on to the lawn.

The staff were already fighting the blaze and endeavouring to rescue the more precious objects of furniture and possessions. It was some time before the calls for help were answered by the local Fire Brigade. In the meantime, clad only in pyjamas and dressing gown, I joined the others with extinguishers and hose in an effort to subdue the conflagration. We had almost succeeded by the time the professionals arrived. As dawn broke, I found Harry Greer despondently assessing the damage. When I went over to him, he looked at me somewhat glumly.

'You know, Porchey, I'm sure you did it for the best but it really is a great pity that in your endeavours to put out the fire you did a great deal more harm than good. A lot of the stuff here has been irretrievably ruined. You know, it's a very serious thing for me, because it would have been much better for the fire to have burned the house down than to have a situation where I cannot claim much and everything is ruined.'

Smoke begrimed and weary, I had to admit to a certain logic in regard to his material possessions, but it did occur to me that he was somewhat ignoring what I should have thought was the first concern of a host.

'Surely, Harry, it would have been a much greater shame if Catherine and I had been burned to death?'

He paused reflectively.

'Yes, I suppose it would,' he said, evidently with some doubt as to the rival merit of the alternatives.

He was one of those men who always agreed with everything said to him about a horse, yet somehow begrudged his final approval. He also had the habit of grunting 'Hm, hm', in an effort not to commit himself to words. I never saw a horse of which he entirely approved. For instance, when visiting my stud, I would take him to the boxes and show him one of my best animals.

'This is quite a good colt, by Blandford. He's rather nice, don't you think?'

'Yes I do: yes, I do: a charming colt. Possibly a little ...'

'Do you mean, er ... a little bit long in his back ...?'

'Well, er ... hm ... er, just a trifle perhaps.'

However Harry Greer was not always non-committal, he could be a very clever salesman. On one occasion, the poor old Aga Khan went to Ireland on his own and Harry showed him two yearlings belonging to the National Stud which were due to be sold at auction. One of them was a chestnut colt by Hurry On out of Ecurie and the other was a colt by Silvern out of Blanche, the dam of Blandford. This was much the better of the two animals.

After an initial inspection in their boxes, Harry turned to the Aga and said, 'It's a great pity, I know, but I really don't see how I can sell you these horses. They are undoubtedly the best yearlings I've ever bred, they're both such beautiful colts. But how can I exclude my two best horses from the batch I'm sending to the sales?'

The spiritual leader of the Ismaili community looked at him perplexed and somewhat astonished.

'But I've come all the way over from England...'

'I know, my dear Aga, I would love to help you, but if I did, I fear I would have to ask you for a lot of money...'

'Well, just say how much,' said the exasperated Aga.

'Well now,' Harry Greer pondered, 'this chestnut colt out of Ecurie, for instance. I think I'd have to say...' he took a deep breath, 'I would have to say ... £20,000.'

The Aga stared at Harry, winced a little, paused. Harry looked contemplative, the very picture of innocence.

'Well, all right, but what about the other ...?'

'Aah,' said Harry, realizing he'd probably managed £20,000 and wondering what else he could extract. 'Now that poses a problem.'

'What's that?' the Aga asked sharply.

'Well, it's not so impeccably bred by comparison with the other one, and I really could not ask you *quite* such a figure, but supposing I was to say £10,000 for that one. Say £30,000 for the two?'

I don't think he dared look at the Aga's face, but studied the ground in front of him.

'Oh, very well,' the Aga agreed and proceeded to write out a cheque on the spot. 'I'd like you to arrange to send them to Dick Dawson at Whatcombe.'

When Dick took delivery and the chestnut colt stepped out of the horse box, he was utterly aghast. Naturally, he knew the details of the transaction and the breeding, but he couldn't believe his eyes as he glanced at him: he was so badly made and extremely straight in front. The Aga, apparently relying entirely on the advice he was being given, had not even asked to have the horses walked out to examine their legs and feet.

At this time, I used to ride work at Whatcombe regularly and even my hack could beat the chestnut Ecurie who never even saw a racecourse. He was eventually sold for ten pounds at public auction in France, but funnily enough, as a stallion he begat quite a few winners.

The less expensive colt named Silver Hussar won the Chesterfield Cup at Goodwood and as I won one thousand pounds on him that day, I have good reason to bless the Aga's purchase.

After this *débacle*, Dick Dawson managed to get the Aga to agree that he would never buy a foal or a yearling without letting him see it first, so long as he was training for him. 'I'll always come and look at it, or Porchey will, because you don't know enough about it, my dear Aga.'

During the years that the Aga trained at Whatcombe with Dick Dawson, I did most of his betting with the help of Cardie Montagu and he had one system from which he never departed. Dick sent the Aga a list each week of his intended runners and stated what chances he thought they had. As Dick was a very cautious man, he usually put 'fair chance' or 'each way chance'. If, on a rare occasion he stuck his neck out and put 'good chance', the Aga always wanted five hundred on the animal, otherwise it was either two hundred to win or one hundred each way.

15
Mug Punting

I saw a lot of my friend Sir Matthew Wilson, known to his friends as Scatters. A great lady-killer, he was constantly engaged in a battle of wits between Barbara, his wife, and Grace Curzon, his steady girlfriend, who was the widow of the late Lord Curzon. She lived near Basingstoke at Hackwood and kept a close check on his movements.

One day he telephoned me to say he had an assignation in town the coming weekend and had told Grace that he was going racing on Saturday and spending the night with me at Highclere.

I told him it was not going to be all that easy for me and what would happen if Grace phoned up asking for him. He said he was sure I'd be able to say *something*, depending on what time of day she called. During the day I could say he was out and in the evening that he was in the middle of a game of bridge and would ring her back.

I said I thought it was all very dicey and I would be caught out if I was not damned careful.

'Go on,' he said, 'you've done it for me before now.'

'Okay, Scatters, but for God's sake tell her that you are arriving late so that I'm not pestered all through the evening.'

'You are a pal, old boy, terribly grateful. I'll do the same for you some day. As a matter of fact, Grace doesn't mind me going to see you. Thinks you're an angel; that's what gave me the idea.'

'I'm very glad to hear that,' I said dryly. 'All right, I'll do the best I can.'

Feeling none too happy about the situation, I briefed my staff. I might have known what would happen. The first call from Lady Curzon came through at about 8.30 p.m. and she was told he was in the middle of dinner.

At ten o'clock the telephone rang again. 'Yes, Lady Curzon. I'll just go and see.' Long gap. 'Hello your ladyship, as a matter of fact he's in the middle of a rubber of bridge. He'll call you directly it is over.'

She called again at 11.30 p.m. to be told Sir Matthew had retired to bed. By lunchtime the following day, she was demanding to speak to me personally and there was no way out of it.

'Hello, my dear Grace. How are you?'

'I'm fine,' she replied, 'but that guest of yours, that dreadful old Scatters; will you please tell him that I've rung him three or four times and so far the beast hasn't rung me back. Where is he?' she asked.

'Oh, how awful. I'm so sorry, he really is the limit. He isn't here, of course...'

'Isn't with you?' she replied very sharply, 'then where is he?'

'I haven't the remotest idea. I suppose he must have left here at about 10.30 ... damned if I can remember where he said he was going.' Suddenly, with inspiration: 'I'll tell you what, Grace, I'm practically certain he'll be in London this evening.'

'Was he in good form?' she asked rather doubtfully.

'Oh marvellous, my dear, marvellous. We played cards, of course, and as usual he pinched all our money.'

Thus I managed to terminate the conversation. Unfortunately, when she telephoned his house in London, she was told that Sir Matthew was still at Highclere. When next I saw

Scatters, I gave him a good ticking off and decided there and then that I would give no more alibis. It was difficult enough to cover one's own tracks without getting involved in another's.

Gamblers have always intrigued me, whether they are playing cards or backing horses. At about this time I became very friendly with a young man called Sidney Beer. He came from Liverpool and we saw a lot of each other, even owned horses in partnership and employed the same solicitor. He loved gambling and while in his company I became friendly with a Greek called George Zographos who ran the baccarat at the Casino in Cannes. He was an imperturbable character who played four 'shoes' daily, two before dinner and two starting just before midnight. Millions of francs changed hands and, on balance, the banker always won. In August he played at Deauville and for the rest of the year he did the same thing in Paris.

However, one day when I was playing a round of golf with him, he said, 'You should never gamble. You have not got the temperament to do so successfully and you look sick with worry when you lose. I strongly advise you to give it up altogether.'

On the other hand, George told me, Sidney was an extremely able gambler and he admired his skill which was in marked contrast to my pitiful performance. I was to remember these comments of his when Catherine and I went to stay at the Carlton Hotel in Cannes with Sidney and his girlfriend Loelia with whom he was madly in love. During the first week Sidney managed to win £60,000 which, in those days, for a young man of his age and not very considerable resources, was a coup of vast proportions. With some difficulty I persuaded him not to gamble any more but to send £50,000 of his winnings to his bank in England.

In the twenties, it was possible to gamble on credit in France, although the law has long since been changed. For instance, Monsieur Citroen might wander in, and murmur '*Cent mille francs à cheval*' which would mean that he was having a hundred thousand francs on each *tableau*. This he was able to do on credit.

Catherine had caught a cold and decided to stay in bed so, after dinner, Sidney, Loelia and I went up to see her. Later Sidney wished to take Loelia dancing but by the time the lift had reached the ground floor, she had told him quite firmly that she would never marry him and went off to her room. Sidney was distraught and spent an hour or two promenading the sea front. Then, reconciling himself to the inevitable, he walked into the casino. George saw him coming and raised his eyebrows, for he knew that I thought I had persuaded him not to gamble again. The money he had already won would have enabled him to buy the racing stables he coveted at Warren Place, which was then on the market for fifty thousand pounds. By the end of the evening, the wheel of fortune had turned full circle: the fifty thousand pounds had disappeared and with it all Sidney's hope of ever purchasing the place.

We had arranged to play tennis the following morning at 10.30 and when I arrived at the courts I found our two opponents waiting but no sign of Sidney. I rang his bedroom and a sleepy voice answered that he was feeling too ill to play and would explain everything to me at lunch. I felt like hitting him hard when I learned the full details.

I spent the rest of that holiday in Cannes forming a lasting friendship with Frank Goldsmith who ran the Carlton Hotel where we were staying. In later years he said to me, 'You know, Porchey, that boy of mine is really something. He's one of those people who, in my opinion, will either become a multi-millionaire or end up in jail.' Happily, Jimmy has successfully accomplished his father's former prediction.

Sidney Beer was not the only person who let vast sums of money slip through his fingers in the thirties. Steve Donoghue also went through a hell of a lot of money as he used to bet like blazes, which was his undoing. He often rode for me; he was a great jockey who never hurt horses and I liked him very much indeed.

Steve was staying at the Grosvenor Hotel, Chester, one time and had just ridden a horse named Our Stephen, after him, which had started a hot favourite for the Chester Cup but been beaten by a short head. Steve had ridden a really good race, but the following morning, when he went down to the barber's shop for a shave, he found himself, unknowingly, at the mercy of a punter who had backed him.

'Well, there's one thing I can tell you, sir, if that little bugger of a jockey, Steve Donoghue, was sitting in this chair now, I'd cut his throat from ear to ear.'

Steve's surprise at this unbridled attack was luckily masked by mountains of lather.

'Why should you say that?' Steve asked him, his eyes twinkling.

'Well, sir, I happened to have had quite a good week in the shop, what with tips and the like, and I decided to back this damned favourite. But I'll tell you this, sir, he wasn't trying – not a yard. Don't suppose he backed it.'

Steve was watching the man intently through the mirror. It was perfectly obvious that he had no idea whom he was shaving.

'Oh,' said Steve in his wonderful manner, 'you mustn't really believe that. I expect he's very keen to ride winners, like any other jockey. He was only beaten a short head.'

Steve found it almost impossible to contain his laughter, but decided that, being at a distinct disadvantage, he would not enlighten the punter whose hand held the cut-throat razor.

Once more my story proves that it is the bookies who always win. One bookie I particularly liked was Joe Pickersgill. He betted entirely to figures. It was the public who made the favourite, he always told me, not the bookmaker. The volume of money decided the odds. Pickersgill died a very rich man. He invested his fortune in property around Leeds and was extremely successful.

He told me that he was always prepared to toss a coin with anybody, but only once, and for any sum up to one thousand pounds. There was one condition. The other person must call to him. The reason, he insisted, was this: the human element was the deciding factor. The other man had to make the decision to call heads or tails whereas all he had to do was to spin the coin. It was even money, but, more often than not, he won.

I myself was always ready to take a gamble, if the odds looked right, but I had no wish to risk my all. About this time two girlfriends played a practical joke on me which I was not easily able to forgive, for it very nearly cost me my life. I was at the height of my riding career and was mad keen to ride anything anywhere.

Catherine was rather unwell that particular morning and I had been out riding alone before breakfast. When I returned, I found that a telegram had been delivered. It read: 'FAWCUS UNABLE TO RIDE TODAY CAN YOU GET LIVERPOOL BY 2.30 THINK HORSE GREAT CHANCE REGARDS SIGNED COULTHWAITE ADELPHI LIVERPOOL.' Tom Coulthwaite was a trainer whom I knew; the horse belonged to Mr Bownas and in the *Sporting Life* that morning, it had been given a very good chance. It was a mile-and-three-quarter race.

I immediately telephoned the firm from whom I usually hired an aeroplane whenever occasion demanded. 'Would it be possible to meet me at Reading by 10.30 in order to fly to Speke where I would pick up a car to take me to the racecourse? I've got to weigh out by 2.15 for the second race.' They told me they thought they could just about manage it, although the weather was not looking too bright. As there was no other way I could possibly be there, I made an instant decision. A Puss Moth and one of their best pilots would take me.

I dashed upstairs, explained the situation to Catherine and left for Reading. The Puss Moth was waiting; I shook hands with the pilot and clambered aboard. Having warmed up the engine, he opened the throttle. The plane bounced over the turf until suddenly we were airborne. We had not been aloft for more than half-an-hour when the weather began to deteriorate. We encountered fierce headwinds and within minutes the clouds seemed to open and the rain descended in torrents. The pilot shouted over the roar of the engine: 'It's a beast of a journey, I'm afraid. I've got to gain as much height as possible to clear these damned hills: then we have the mountains in front of us. Unfortunately, I'm no longer absolutely sure where the hell I am and I'll have to ask you to help me. Can you open your window and keep a sharp look-out? Search for any features you can see through the cloud layer. It's a pretty tricky situation.'

He had no need to explain. By now I was thoroughly frightened for, in those days, navigation was purely by compass, with no other aids whatsoever. We bucketed and lurched through the air, with occasional streaks of lightning and horrifying thunder. The wings seemed unutterably fragile and I felt sick. This to me looked like the end as I failed to see how the pilot could ever get down.

For an hour we kept ploughing our way forward, the pilot calling every now and again asking if I had managed to see anything.

'I can't see a bloody thing,' I kept yelling in response, each time feeling ever more frightened.

'Well, we should be over the mountains by now,' he shouted, 'for God's sake tell me when you first catch a glimpse of the sea. Our margin of fuel is dwindling but we've still a little time left.'

With the slipstream tearing at my face, I peered anxiously below, but could see nothing. Ten minutes later he shouted again.

'It's no good, I'm going to have to take her lower down. I'm sure on my time reckoning that by now we must be over the Irish Sea. For God's sake keep your eyes skinned and if you should see any sign of a hill, hit me on the shoulder and I'll try to get her up again.'

'What a bloody fool I am,' I thought to myself, 'all for the 2.30 race at Liverpool.'

For another ten minutes we buffeted our way westwards until, through a gap in the clouds, I saw the rain-lashed ocean.

'The sea!' I yelled in ecstasy, 'the sea!' and punched him as hard as I could.

'Thank God for that,' I heard the pilot murmur and pushing the stick forward, he took us down rapidly. Beneath the cloud layer we easily made out the coast and found that we had only just passed over Liverpool. Banking steeply, we descended towards Speke and made an excellent landing. I congratulated my saviour and rewarded him accordingly.

I arrived just after two to see Steve Donoghue coming in, having won the first race. I rushed into the weighing room to change.

'Take it easy,' he said, 'you've got five minutes at least to weigh out.'

Jack Clayton hurried in looking very worried. As he caught sight of me, a wave of relief swept over his face.

'Oh, Lordy, thank God you're safe,' he began, 'believe me we did everything to stop you, everything, but I'm afraid it was too late.'

'Why, what on earth's the matter?' I asked him.

'Well,' he said, gulping and trying to summon up enough courage to tell me, 'you see, Lordy dear, it was a practical joke. At midnight last night M and the rest of the gang decided to pull your leg. We never thought you'd take it seriously. Tried to stop you at Reading. A man ran out waving a red flag, but your pilot never saw him. Terribly sorry, it was a stupid practical joke.'

I felt physically sick. At this moment Coulthwaite rushed in, having obviously heard the story.

'Lord Carnarvon, the owner, Jack Fawcus and I, we all beg you to ride our horse. Want you to do it, you're on a good thing; certain to win and I've made the necessary arrangements. It's going to sock the hell out of these people who have played this miserable trick.' He was white with anger.

Then Fawcus, the original rider, walked in: 'Go on,

Porchey. I'm delighted to stand down. I want you to take the ride.'

For a moment I hesitated, then somewhat reluctantly replied, 'No, honestly, a million thanks, but after this experience, I wouldn't do the horse justice. Anyway, it's your ride, you take it.'

Ill as I was feeling, I nevertheless went out immediately in search of a bookie and put two hundred pounds on the horse. He won in a canter. I returned to London by train with Monica, Jack and all the others and forty-eight hours later I received a most charming letter from 'Flash' Kellett enclosing a cheque for £175 to cover the expense of the plane. I tore it up. On Sunday, most of the newspapers had the story in great detail and, as a result, many offers to ride came in from all over the country, even from trainers I did not know.

Another character I knew who had made and lost a fortune – and made it again – was Sir Hugo Cunliffe-Owen, Bt, of German extraction. He ended up by becoming chairman of the British American Tobacco company. His second wife, Helen, was a close friend of Catherine's, both of them being American, and frequently stayed at Highclere. Helen was mad about racing and gambled very heavily. This contagious disease she transmitted to Catherine and, at the time, I had no idea of its proportions.

Hugo had a house at Newmarket, at which we were frequently guests, and a little house on the banks of the Thames at Bray. He usually had three or four Great Danes. One day, dear little Helen wandered into the garden in the early afternoon, walked down to the riverbank and lost her balance and toppled into the deep water of the Thames. She was alone and could not swim. Coming to the surface and threshing about, she screamed for help. It was their black Great Dane, Mutton, who answered her cries.

Racing down the lawn, the dog leapt into the water, swam to his mistress, grabbed her hair in his mouth and proceeded to drag her ashore. It was a remarkable example of an animal having an acute ability to understand the need of its master or mistress.

Hugo owned a filly called Scotford in partnership with his Australian trainer de Mestre who, at one time, trained for Solly Joel. He was a hard man with horses, somewhat cruel but nevertheless quite successful. The filly was entered in the Queen Mary Stakes at Royal Ascot and also running was a filly owned by the Aga called Qurrat-Al-Ain. Qurrat-Al-Ain had made her debut at Newmarket and I had backed her heavily. My commission had been done by Jack Clayton and she won. Afterwards, I said to him, 'This filly will win the Queen Mary,' to which he replied, 'That's a very far cry but I'll be happy to lay you four to one at this stage.'

'Right,' said I, 'I'll have a monkey on her.'

'You've got it,' he replied.

When it came to Ascot, I was somewhat concerned as to the damage my bet might inflict on dear Jack who was one of my greatest friends.

'Look here, Jack, this filly is going awfully well and I think she's a good thing. Please put me on another thousand.'

'Okay, Lordy dear, I certainly will.'

'And for God's sake, Jack, cover that bet of yours; I don't want you to end up having a bad race.'

The filly opened round about evens and in order to do any good Jack had to have about five thousand pounds on her. I found out afterwards he had had ten thousand. Scotford was ridden by Cecil Ray and Qurrat-Al-Ain by Michael Beary.

They were off and my heart stood still, for Beary was left a couple of lengths at the start. Endeavouring to make up lost ground, Beary was forced to ride her hard, giving her several smacks. He managed to catch up but was only able to draw level with Scotford in the last hundred yards. Beary knew he was cooked. However, he was suddenly offered a last chance which he took. The two fillies were level, stride for stride. By a cunning manœuvre, Beary found he was just able to get his right knee over Cecil Ray's left and, as his rival tried desperately to move forward, Beary held him back with every ounce of strength he could command. Then, at the very last moment, he inched Qurrat-Al-Ain forward to win by a short head.

De Mestre had seen what had happened and told Cunliffe-Owen, who was furiously angry. Helen, luckily, had had an enormous wager on Qurrat-Al-Ain. Seeing that her husband was going to lodge an objection, she caught up with him and addressed him in the following manner.

'Hugo, listen to me. I'll leave you ... I'll never speak to you again ... I'll leave your house, I'll leave you and the children, everything, if you dare to object. Jack Clayton has had his all on Qurrat-Al-Ain and I have also. We're all on her up to the hilt, including Porchey. This is not an occasion for you to start any of your tricks. If you do, you'll be the most unpopular man on earth. Now, *stop it! stop it!*' she ordered.

Hugo came to a halt at this tirade and, furious as he was, there was no doubting that his wife meant all that she had said. He looked at her sadly and only spoke two words before walking away: 'You win.'

Hugo's luck was a close-run thing on more than one occasion in which I was involved. He was always dabbling in new ventures and one day he said to me, 'I know you're rather fond of jewellery and you know a lot about it. I've had a bit of luck and I've managed to purchase a large, square-cut emerald that has been smuggled into this country by one of the Russian *émigrés*. By all accounts, it is supposed to have been the property of Tsar Nicholas. I believe I've bought it very cheaply and I thought you might care to sell it on my behalf. If you can do so, we shall split the profit fifty-fifty.'

'Interesting,' I said, 'but first, before I say yea or nay, what weight is it and how much did you pay?'

'Around twenty carats and I paid twenty thousand pounds.'

In due course I examined the stone through my glass and found what I had feared. It was certainly an excellent colour but, upon close scrutiny, I discovered that it had quite a lot of 'silk'.

'What do you think?' he asked.

'Very difficult to say, my dear Hugo. I wouldn't say it was cheap. It's by no means perfect. However, if you'd like to leave the ring with me, I'll do what I can.'

'How much do you think we'll make?' he urged, 'ten thousand pounds?'

'Good God, no, it will be nothing like that. If we clear a thousand, we'll be damned lucky.'

'Then I've boobed?'

'Well, I wouldn't say boobed but I wouldn't have bought it myself. These dealers are cunning fellows and, as you know nothing about jewels, they have taken you for a ride.'

However, anxious to help Hugo, I set to immediately and contacted my friends in the trade. Their reaction was not encouraging, and the more I tried, the less I succeeded. I decided to have one final go. I had known an old Jewish dealer off and on for years. He was rather fond of racing and owned one or two horses that were trained by Sir Charles Nugent at Lambourn. Old Charlie Nugent was as hot as hell and had a habit of getting up extraordinarily early in the morning so that he could gallop his horses when no touts were about.

I explained the situation to my friend in Hatton Garden. He replied that I was crazy to dabble in a market in which I was by no means an expert.

'It's not a bad sort of stone; I agree it's got good colour, but it is nothing special. I'll tell you what I'll do. I'll give you eighteen thousand pounds for it.'

'Eighteen thousand!' I echoed with a horrified expression on my face, although this offer was somewhat better than I had received so far, 'how on earth can I go back to Sir Hugo and tell him he has made a loss?'

'Well, I'm not a charitable institution, my lord, and if he *will* pay over the odds...'

'Can't you do a little better than that?'

He thought for a few minutes then suddenly seemed to have an inspiration.

'Tell you what I'll do. I've got a horse called Illuminator running in the Hunt Cup and Charlie Nugent thinks it's got a pretty good chance. If we're lucky and he wins, I'll give you twenty-one thousand for this ruddy emerald.'

'I've had some curious deals in my time but what racing has to do with the sale of an emerald I'm damned if I know.' Thoroughly fed up with the whole business, I made up my mind: 'All right, it's a deal.'

I left his office and returned home to study the form of the runners in the Hunt Cup. The best I could make of Illuminator was that he had an outside chance. Nevertheless, having committed myself so far, I thought the obvious thing to do was to put fifteen pounds on him. My only real hope was that I knew Charlie to be a shrewd operator. Happily Illuminator won and was returned at fifty to one against. I had £1000 to £15 with Issy Isaacs. I was delighted to have sold the emerald and come out with a profit.

As I have said, under the influence of Helen Cunliffe-Owen, my darling wife had also developed a great taste for betting. One fine day in the autumn of 1924, a filly called Saucy Sue belonging to Waldorf Astor was running in the Chieveley Park Stakes. There were very few runners and as she was an outstanding mare, the bookies were offering to take seven to two. I was standing chatting to friends near the rails when Issy Isaacs called me over. He very often gave me a good cigar.

'Would you like to do something?'

'Right. What?'

'Have a cigar.'

'Thanks.'

'Her ladyship has laid me £7,000 to £2,000 on Saucy Sue and she might like to hedge her bet.'

Saucy Sue was then six to one on and Isaacs suggested that he should lay her six thousand to one on. She would then be in the happy position of having an even thousand. I ran off to find Catherine and rapidly explained the position to her.

'As far as I can understand this business,' she replied, 'if Saucy Sue wins I'm only going to win a thousand. As I'm certain she will win, I shall keep my bet as it is and win two thousand.'

I returned to Issy with the somewhat difficult task of trying to explain Catherine's logic. Neither Issy nor I need have bothered. Saucy Sue won easily and the following year won the Oaks.

Catherine had two other spectacular wins before beginner's luck finally eluded her. She laid £11,000 to £8,000 on Manna and he trotted up. Another large bet of hers was when she laid £12,000 to £8,000 on a very good horse called Picaroon, who duly obliged at Kempton. But after that it became a very different story and it was with horror that I eventually learned that the tiara my father had given to her as a wedding present had been accepted by Arthur Bendir in settlement of her debts. Thereafter, she ceased betting. Poor darling, it had been a very hard lesson.

Some time later Hugo Cunliffe-Owen invited me to lunch with him before Royal Ascot at a house he had taken near Swinley Golf Course. During lunch he explained, 'After the first race I shall be bringing three distinguished Chinese gentlemen into the weighing room. I wonder if you would be so good as to show them around and explain the various procedures?' Strictly speaking, one was not supposed to take guests into this area but as I was very well-known, he thought that few questions would be asked.

I had just won a thousand pounds on Diolite in the first race and was feeling full of good cheer. I waited in the weighing room as requested and, in due course, Hugo came in with his three Chinese guests. They were immaculately turned out in top hats and tails. They bowed graciously and, during the introductions, I heard myself speaking pidgin English to them. What on earth made me do it, I shall never know.

'You likee see weighing room? I show you velly, velly interesting things.'

Vague shadows seemed to flit across their faces. They bowed again and in another torrent of words I continued, 'All flee come along with me.'

As I turned to lead the way, I heard one of them say, in a perfect Oxford accent, 'How extraordinary that Lord Carnarvon should talk to us in pidgin English. He must think we are very curious people.'

This remark could have had no more devastating effect upon me than if he had thrown a bucket of cold water in my face. Had the earth opened up and swallowed me, I would have counted it a blessing. I have seldom felt more ashamed. Fortunately, at that moment, Hugo caught me up and I fled. I kept out of their way for the rest of the afternoon.

16
The Letter

Of course, I ought not to have been surprised but, nevertheless, it still came as a shattering blow. I was returning from a visit to Deauville; it was Sunday and a peaceful summer evening. I looked through the open car window awaiting the first glimpse of Highclere. Everything was serene. As always, I looked forward to my homecoming and as the car stopped, I stepped briskly into the Castle.

'Where is her ladyship?' I asked my butler.

There was a momentary pause. His eyes flickered and he avoided my gaze. Immediately I sensed that something was wrong.

'I believe her ladyship is staying at the Ritz Hotel,' he said, trying to impart the information with neither emotion nor undue concern. There was another pause and I did not take my eyes off him.

'What an extraordinary thing, on a Sunday...?'

'There is a letter on your desk, my lord,' and with that he bowed politely, as if indicating that he wished to be questioned no further.

I went to my study with mixed thoughts running through my head. My hands were unsteady as I opened the envelope. The words that leapt from the sheets gradually became blurred: '... cannot go on ... better we should part ... must have peace of mind ... not really accustomed to this way of life. I have made up my mind irrevocably.' I dropped into my chair behind my desk, the full import sinking in. I felt utterly miserable.

Twenty minutes elapsed before I reached for the phone. Catherine sounded cool and collected, and already she was becoming a stranger.

I said, 'Let me come up and bring you back so that we can talk it all over. I'm sure there must be a solution...'

'No Porchey, I have made up my mind. Come up and see me by all means, but I am not returning. Leave it until tomorrow.'

'Very well,' I murmured despondently, 'good night, my love.'

I was terribly upset. Faults on both sides, of course; mine by far the worse. The frailty of human nature...

We met at the Ritz and Catherine said, 'Let's have no scandal. I shall divorce you. My brother Jack will take care of my interests. I well know how generous and kind you are so I am quite content to leave all the arrangements to you.'

There was no more to be said. I walked out into Piccadilly feeling intolerably sad.

17

Betwixt and Between

Among our close-knit circle of friends there was always considerable discussion on the merits of the leading trainers and Cardy Montagu and I used to make a handicap at the end of each season to assess their relative positions. This was a light-hearted exercise in which the trainers themselves participated and found amusing. Fred Darling was always top weight with twelve stone seven, after whom came Frank Butters, Dick Dawson and George Lambton; there was never any great controversy as to how the various trainers were handicapped. Harry Rosebery once said to me, 'Good God! I must say I don't agree with you. You've got Jack Jarvis at least three pounds too low.' Jack, of course, was Lord Rosebery's own trainer and a staunch friend of both Harry and myself. However, after a number of years, this little game came to an unfortunate conclusion.

One fine day at Newmarket, I was idly looking at the horses before the first race when a certain trainer, one of the somewhat lesser lights in the fraternity, came up to me and said, 'Excuse me, Lord Carnarvon, may I have a quick word with you?'

'Certainly,' I replied, 'very nice to see you. What's on your mind?'

At this point he produced a copy of our latest trainers' handicap which he thrust under my nose. I did not need to read it to know that his was the last name on the list.

'Am I really as bad as that?' he asked me pointedly.

'Good Heavens, no,' I said, trying my hardest to make light of his placement, 'you know as well as I do that it's only a silly little game.'

'It may be a game to you and your friends, m'lord, but it certainly isn't to me. And I'll tell you why. A few weeks ago, one of my patrons, a wealthy Jew, commissioned me to buy him two or three yearlings at the Houghton sales and he was prepared to spend big money. When I next met him, he stuck your list under my nose and said he was not going to train with me and buy yearlings for me to ruin. He went on to say that he was going to pick one of the better trainers on the list.'

To say that I was horrified would be a major understatement; I almost burst into tears when I realized how damaging had been our little bit of fun. Whereas for years everyone had taken it in very good part, it had now backfired. After offering my most profuse apologies, I hurried to find Cardie. We decided there and then that we would never do it again. The last thing we had expected was that anyone might take the placings seriously.

This unfortunate occurrence had taken place at Newmarket, the headquarters of English racing. I took Max Beaverbrook there for his first visit and was disconcerted by his reactions. Max and I had many mutual friends, among them Brendan Bracken, Valentine Castleross, Diana and Duff Cooper; on many occasions I had stayed with Max at Cherkley and we'd all gossiped half through the night. Indeed in the early days of our friendship, I had even introduced the Beaver to one of my girlfriends. She complained bitterly thereafter. 'Do you know what?' she told me, 'when we're in bed together Max insists on reading two or three chapters from the Bible; it's terribly boring.'

Max, of course, was very opinionated, and he had a trick of asking questions to which he already knew the answers.

An example of this occurred when I took him on this, his first visit to Newmarket.

'Now, tell me Porchey, what is this, a five furlong race?' (He knew perfectly well that it was.) 'And the horses that are going down now. Will they start over there by that post – is that right?'

'Yes, it is,' I replied.

'Aha,' he said, 'and they will come as fast as they can and finish up here?'

'That's right.'

He paused, looking round with distaste.

'A very windswept place, this Newmarket. Most unpleasant. Now, tell me some more. These stands seem very old-fashioned; they look very bleak and I don't see all that many people.'

'Well, I'm afraid that's the trouble, my dear Max.'

'Yet this is the headquarters of English racing,' he said dramatically. 'Well, I can understand why they don't get many people. The catering is extremely bad. No doubt the quality of the turf is good?'

'Even that, my dear Max, rather depends on the weather.'

'Quite so, yeah, well if you want my opinion, this place is grossly over-rated.'

Max was an astute person in many ways, one whose opinion I greatly valued, if not in this case. Another friend who was equally astute was my brother-in-law, Eve's husband, Bro Beauchamp. One day in the late thirties, he came to me and said, 'I wonder if you'd be interested in seeing a tiny little factory on the outskirts of Paris where, at present, they are employing only three people. They have developed a copper cable which is completely fire-proof. It has been absolutely proven and I'm told that if we go over there, they will demonstrate it. It will make all electrical wiring safe and obviate the common problem of overheated wires setting fire to houses.

'One of the ideas is that it should be used in submarines. The rights are held by a Pole whose name is Jean Horodyski.

This chap is a fascinating character and, I am told, worked for us as a spy in the last war. He's also a gourmet, so you'll have something in common.

'For instance, I believe that once a year he goes to Switzerland just to eat mountain trout when they reach the peak of perfection. Or then again, he may go to the south of France to catch the peaches at the moment they reach their best and the ortolans that have been feeding on vine leaves and have such an exquisite flavour.

'Anyway, I understand he might be persuaded to sell the European rights in his invention. I've got a hunch it could be an enormous money-spinner. How about it?'

We duly went to Paris together and I met Horodyski who was known as 'Le Polonais'. He was rotund, as might be expected, cherubic and cheerful. I liked him immensely. We were taken to his factory where a sample of the cable was measured with a pair of callipers and then placed in a white hot furnace which was then clamped shut and we sealed it with Bro's signet ring. Twenty-four hours later we returned. The cable was extracted and plunged into a bucket of cold water. When measured again, it had changed not one millimetre.

'Well, Lordy dear, what do you think of it?' Bro asked me.

'Marvellous, absolutely marvellous! Whether it will be the success you believe I have no way of knowing, but I hope you will be right.'

'Do you want to come in?'

'Of course I want to come in. How much?'

'Well, Horodyski wants £125,000 for the European rights. I would like to keep it as small as possible and only do it with pals. How much would you like to invest?'

'I don't know, whatever you want. £10,000? £15,000? Just tell me and I'll send you a cheque.'

In due course my brother-in-law worked out the percentage between us and I paid him £12,000. A pilot plant was set up. Later on, our factory started up in Newcastle. From the beginning, all went well and from the declaration of war in 1939 onwards the factory produced as much cable as could be made from the copper available, though no profits could be taken because of wartime restrictions. After the war, a free issue of shares was made and Pyrotenax became a name to conjure with. Bro managed our affairs so well that I, being one of the original syndicate, collected thousands of additional shares until the day came when the company was due to go public.

'How much do you think our shares are worth, dear Bro?' I asked him.

'I've no idea,' he told me, 'but you haven't done badly, have you?'

'Badly! It's been fantastic.'

'Now, Porchey, I want to make a pool so that we've got some ammunition for the jobbers, and I suggest we all chip in ten per cent which we must be prepared to sell at a minimum of thirty shillings each. Anything above that figure we share pro rata.'

'Fair enough.'

When dealing began, there was pandemonium in the Stock Exchange. A number of brokers clawed and scratched in their mad rush to deal and halfway through the morning, a leading jobber rang up my broker, Reggie Rogers: 'Look here, you know Carnarvon. Do you think you could persuade him to part with more shares? If he'll agree, I'll send him a dozen magnums of Bollinger.'

Rogers rang me up and I agreed to sell another fifty thousand shares, but in so doing I made a very grave error. The company went from strength to strength until, finally, it was sold to BICC. I held on a little longer, but when I eventually sold all my holding, I found that my original twelve thousand pounds had made me over three hundred thousand net profit. Undoubtedly, this was my best killing.

18
Hamman Meeting

When we were both very young, at the end of the First World War, I saw a great deal of George v's eldest son, the Prince of Wales, as we used to go down to Gil Bennett's place at Epsom and ride work. I also hunted with him in Leicestershire. He was a fearless rider but I thought his horses were frequently out of control as he was inclined to jab them in the mouth for he did not have the best of hands.

The Prince of Wales was not a good shot. One rather amusing incident took place when we were partridge shooting at Laverstoke with Wyndham Portal. That particular day, we had an enormous number of birds to shoot at and Harry Brown was on one side of the Prince and I on the other. We were shooting as fast as our loaders could hand us the guns when the Prince, having missed a great many, put his gun down and walked away in the middle of the drive, so Harry and I closed the gap, calling on Godfrey Miller-Mundy to come nearer to us. Both of them were very good shots. After lunch, the 'little man' left for London in something of a huff! That day, we established a record for partridges in Hampshire.

I saw a good deal of the Prince throughout his life and later when he became Edward VIII we often played golf together at home and abroad. It was on one of these golfing sprees that I first met Wallis; we all lunched on the Lido at Venice with Eric Dudley. I was intrigued by His Majesty's obvious devotion to this good lady of whom I had heard a great deal.

After lunch a friend who was in the party took me aside and said to me, 'I think you should try to explain to your dear friend that he has not been given very good advice by Duff and Winston. People have more or less told him that if he marries Wallis, he will probably get away with it – even if she has to be his morganatic wife. I am sure that this will not be the case and I don't want to see him hurt beyond repair. Forgive me for saying this to you, but I know you are great friends and have known each other a long time.' I got the impression that day that Wallis did not take kindly to me, nor I to her. I think she felt that I would be unlikely to encourage their association, which was indeed the case.

I was at Highclere when Ulick Alexander called me up and said that George, Duke of Kent, would be very grateful if I would go and see him at Belgrave Square the following morning by 11 a.m. When I asked if it was in connection with the Monarch he said it was. I motored up to London the following day and found Prince George or P.G. as we called him, in a highly nervous state. Although usually affectionate and full of good humour, he was now obviously rattled and started by saying, 'Marina is upstairs and won't disturb us. My family is absolutely distraught, we feel convinced that David* intends to abdicate as Baldwin has made it clear that *she* will not be accepted as Queen. A morganatic marriage will not be tolerated either. However, David is hell-bent on marrying her, so I think it is highly probable that he will go and marry her somewhere abroad. We may all be hanging from lamp-posts shortly, as there is bound to be a tremendous outcry in the country and a violent reaction to the monarchy in general.'

I told him that I did not agree with his suggestion that the

*Although the Prince of Wales became Edward VIII, he was called David by his family.

royal family would be in any danger or become unpopular, because I knew that many of them were very dear to the hearts of the British people as, indeed, Edward VIII had been for years. To me he was so full of charm that I did not believe his image could ever become tarnished. Had it not been for his taking a rather unwarranted interest in political matters and particularly in foreign policy which eventually brought him into contact with Hitler, it seemed to me that his popularity would have remained unimpaired.

P.G. then suggested to me that as his brother and I had been such great friends for so long, I ought to have one last go at making him see reason. I asked him what he wished me to do.

'My family and I – and that includes my mother – want you to go and meet David in the hot room at the Hammam in Jermyn Street tomorrow morning. He will be there about 7.30 a.m. and we want you to be there at least half-an-hour before him. It has been arranged that nobody except the usual masseurs will be in the place between 7 and 9 a.m. I suggest that you should tell him, quite frankly, that there is no chance whatsoever of his remaining on the throne if he insists on marrying this woman. So, we leave it to you to make one last attempt and, even if it fails, we shall all be tremendously grateful to you for trying.'

The following morning I went to the steam room and after five minutes in the steam, I went and sat in one of the canvas deck-chairs in the hot room. In those days, the room was really hot and I was sweating freely when Edward VIII entered; I scrambled to my feet; both of us were stark naked. He started the ball rolling by saying, 'Lovely to see you! I wonder if you are here by accident or design? Anyway, sit down and tell me what is on your mind.'

'Sir,' I replied, 'you are quite correct in thinking that I am here by design.'

'I suppose my brother, George, asked you to come and see me?' he enquired.

I told him this was the case.

'Well, I expect I know what it's all about, but let's hear your views.'

I told him I was convinced he was physically infatuated. At that he replied, 'That old fool, Baldwin, said the same thing to me yesterday but, my dear Porchey, this is not the case! I am absolutely devoted to Wallis and she is a necessary adjunct to my life and I cannot do without her.'

'Have you realized fully that you are about to sell your birthright for a mess of pottage?'

'How dare you call her a mess of pottage!'

I quickly explained that my meaning was entirely biblical but I have always felt that he enjoyed that touch of humour in what was really a tragic moment for both of us. He assured me that nothing would stop him: he was determined to marry Wallis and would broadcast this to the nation, telling us that he felt sure his brother Bertie would make an excellent king, particularly as he had the good fortune to have a charming wife and family. Before he left, he asked me to come and stay with him in Austria after his wedding. I did not do so.

I did, however, go to Paris to spend a couple of days with them both. I stayed at the Ritz and they were at the Meurice. This visit had a somewhat unfortunate ending. I gave a dinner party for them at Maxims and invited two American friends and Daria Mercati. They were both in splendid form and, after a very good dinner and plenty to drink, HRH the Duke of Windsor said, 'Now, Porchey, to crown our happy evening, please do some of your famous impersonations, such as the one of our dear friend Burghey or Winston, or – always my favourite – the Christmas Day broadcast that my father used to do every year.'

Except for the waiters hovering about and two Englishmen sitting some distance away smoking cigars, the place was empty, so I carried on with the imitations. Everybody hooted with laughter and I ended by giving King George v's Buckingham Palace broadcast which always delighted his son. Shortly after that the two Englishmen left the restaurant and, after paying the bill, I said good-night to them all and went home to bed.

A week later I was summoned to see P.G. at Belgrave Square. Wondering what on earth this was about, I entered the well-known portals, was escorted upstairs and told that HRH the Duke of Kent would soon be with me. A furious figure stalked into the room and this is exactly what he said. 'I really cannot understand how you – of all people – could make a mockery of my family at Maxims to please my brother and his wife.'

I stared at him for a moment and then enquired how on earth the story had come to his ears.

'Very simply,' he replied, 'one of our Embassy staff and a friend witnessed the whole of this performance of yours. He was horrified at the unseemly way in which my brother responded to your act and reported the whole thing to the Foreign Office who, in turn, have told me what occurred.'

I explained that I had not meant the slightest harm to anybody but agreed that if I had done the impersonations at all, I should have done them in private. However, one does not always act as one should! I consoled myself with Harry Rosebery's words when I saw him in White's and told him about being ticked off by P.G.

'My dear Porchey, people have short memories. Don't worry, you have been a good friend to them all for so long that none of them will hold it against you.'

I am happy to say that none of them ever did.

Catherine had just remarried and, sensing that the Second World War was imminent, I felt lonely and depressed and above all wanted congenial companionship. Whilst in this frame of mind, I was delighted to learn that Tilly Losch was staying with Michael Duff at Vaynol.

I had first met Tilly some years before at a party in New York, given by Jules Bache, when one of his guests, Charles Cavendish, passed out. Fred Astaire's sister, Adele, was ministering to the unfortunate victim, whom she subsequently married, with the help of Tilly and, after we had revived him, I was introduced to this ravishing girl who had been a ballet dancer, stage actress and screen star. I invited her to dance and she informed me that I was unlike most Englishmen she had met who usually had no sense of rhythm and stood on her toes. I basked in these compliments for the rest of the evening and our friendship developed rapidly.

When she came to England, I invited her to Highclere and she came with Leslie Hore-Belisha, who said to me that he thought she would make a marvellous châtelaine of Highclere. 'She's so graceful, accomplished, divinely pretty, and those hands ... they are filled with expression,' he said, all of which was perfectly true and the whole image was enhanced by a soft continental accent. Her father was a Polish Jew from Lodz and, upon arrival in Vienna, had taken the name of Losch. Tilly at the age of three or four had taken the first steps in what was to prove a highly successful dancing career, for she eventually joined the ranks of the Imperial Ballet.

Her mother was a Catholic and her brother a cavalry officer who had been killed in the First World War. She remembered only too clearly the deprivations the family had suffered in war-time Vienna and the horrors Hitler was already perpetrating against the Jewish population undoubtedly terrified her.

Tilly had a very great friend who acted *in loco parentis*. His name was Rudolph Kommer, an Austrian Jew who was steeped in the theatre. He acted as a talent scout for C.B. Cochran and there wasn't a person in films or in the theatre that he did not know.

When in London, he had a table permanently reserved for him at the Ritz; in New York at the Colony Restaurant; in Paris it was the Ritz again and nearly every day he gave a luncheon party to which people from all walks of life were invited. He was an ugly man but Tilly was very fond of him and he of her. It was Kommer who rather approved of the idea that we might marry although I doubt if this was openly discussed with her.

I was returning from America aboard the *Normandy* and knew that Tilly was spending six weeks in Wales. I sent her a cable from the ship asking her to join me for dinner on my arrival in London. She replied: DELIGHTED DINE LOVE TILLY.' She was staying at Claridges and I at the Ritz. She was looking beautiful and after we had dined, I popped the question.

We could hardly have been described as head over heels in love. After all, I had known her on and off for quite a number of years and neither of us were in the prime of our youth. Tilly had been married to Arthur James and he had cited Serge Obolensky in his divorce suit.

'Porchey dear,' she said, 'it's simply divine and flattering of you to ask me and I know you would not wish me to make an immediate decision, would you? Firstly, I would want to see very much more of you and talk about many things. I would also like to consult Kommer for I must think very carefully before I give you an answer. There's another thing; I'm very frightened of this impending war. My mother lives in America and I may have to go back to be with her.'

With Tilly's practical mind obviously hard at work, I cast around to make a worthwhile suggestion.

'I've an idea,' I said, 'look, darling, you love Paris and so do I. Why don't we go over to Paris for a couple of weeks and have a little quiet fun on our own. It would help us to get to know each other better.'

Tilly looked up sharply.

'No, nothing of that sort,' she told me, 'that's not my idea at all. I'll promise you one thing, you'll not be disappointed by waiting. The idea of going to Paris is appealing, but you will stay at the Ritz and I shall stay at my hotel.'

'Just as you like.'

We went to Paris and had only been there one night when it was announced that general mobilization was taking place in France. We hurriedly booked our seats to return home. It looked very much as if the inevitable was shortly to happen.

Poor Tilly was seasick on the way back.

'Now what are we going to do?' I asked her.

'I am going away for three days and nights alone and during that time I don't wish you to contact me. I need time to think. When I come back, I shall give you my decision. If it's in the affirmative then I think we should get married straight away.'

'Very well,' I said, 'to-day's Monday, we'll meet again on Thursday.'

'I'm sure that's right, darling, I don't want to make another mistake.'

After we had parted, I gave the matter much thought and asked my solicitor what would have to be done. I learnt that we would require a special licence, so I made the necessary application. In order to keep the press hounds at bay, I decided to apply using Tilly's married name, Ethel Ottilie James and my family name, Henry George Herbert. I gave my address as the Ritz and her address as Claridges.

But fate, in the form of a bright reporter, struck me a severe blow. As a routine measure, his paper insisted that the reporter should check the marriage registers each week. What it was that caught his attention I shall never know; perhaps our hotel addresses, or then again the unusual name of Ottilie, from which Tilly was derived. His curiosity aroused, the man returned to his office and consulted the clippings library.

The registry had revealed that both persons had been divorced so he asked if they had any records of Mrs Ethel Ottilie James. Greatly excited, his perception rewarded, Tilly's name was uncovered, but not mine. The reporter took a taxi to the Ritz and asked George Kriticos, the hall porter, whether there was a gentleman staying there by the name of Mr Herbert. The porter consulted Reception and they confirmed that no-one of that name was staying there.

The reporter looked sceptical and puzzled.

'Well, would it be helpful if I explained that we believe he has a friend called Mrs James who is known to everyone as the famous Tilly Losch?'

'Oh, Miss Losch. Yes, she comes here regularly to see Lord Carnarvon.'

It was front page news in the next edition.

I had gone down to Brighton races and when I returned to the Ritz I found a message awaiting me. Tilly was back at Claridges; would I go round immediately? It was the evening of 31 August 1939, hot and humid, and I found Tilly in a great state of agitation. With her, to my surprise, was our friend Sidney.

'Have you see the papers?' she enquired. 'The special licence, did you manage to get it?'

'Yes, it has all been arranged. If you're quite happy about it, we can be married in the morning.'

'Well, I've been discussing it with Sidney,' she confided, 'and I haven't yet made up my mind. You see, there are many cons and very few pros.'

'Well then, there's no more to be said.'

'Don't be so beastly,' she replied, 'I didn't mean that. I expressed myself badly. My darling Porchey, what I'm trying to say is this. I don't want to be in England if there's going to be a war; and then there's the question of my health. As you know, I've got a bad lung and I've been warned by my doctor that I must find a dry climate for the winter. He suggested Arizona but, if there is a war, shall I be able to get there?'

'How can I possibly answer that?'

'Well, there are many, many factors,' she told me, looking round to Sidney for support. 'I do like you very much indeed but I'm not in love with you. However, Sidney thinks it would be a very good idea and so does Kommer.'

'I'm very glad to hear that,' I said, 'but on the other hand, you seem so undecided that I'm beginning to have grave doubts.'

'Porchey, do you still want to marry me?'

'Yes!'

'All right, if you really do, I will.'

'Don't make a favour of it! It seems to me as if you don't know what you want to do.'

'Oh, it's very difficult for me to explain properly,' she said. 'What do you think, Sidney?'

'For God's sake, Tilly, make up your mind one way or the other! We cannot go on like this all night.'

'Well, tell him about the question of money for me,' she said.

'Money?' I echoed, 'what's money got to do with it?'

'Well,' said Sidney, looking flustered, 'Tilly feels that she ought to have some kind of financial security – nothing substantial, but at least an agreed annual income that she can really call her own. She feels that if you could give your formal approval to a document guaranteeing her a thousand a year, she will feel much happier. Can that be done?'

I looked at the pair of them.

'It can't be done right now, if that's what you mean.'

'No, I know it can't be done now but your solicitor could draw up a document to be signed and I can witness it as soon as the ceremony is over. Tilly just wants to feel that if anything should happen to you, or you should leave her, at least she's got something to live on.'

I thought this reasonable and rang up my solicitor.

'Everything seems okay,' I told him and then I mentioned the settlement.

'Very good, I shall draw it up, but I shall be inserting one clause . . . 'so long as she remains your wife and you are living in conjugal bliss', otherwise you will be entering into a commitment in perpetuity and that I could never approve.'

I went back to Tilly's room.

'All set for 9.30 tomorrow morning,' I told her. 'I'm starving, we've been at this for two and a half hours and all I've had is a tepid Scotch. Let's go out and get a meal.'

Sidney excused himself, suggesting we should spend the

evening alone. When we walked into the Savoy Grill at 9.30 p.m. I saw two of my closest friends sitting at a table having had dinner by themselves – Duff Cooper and Crinks Harcourt Johnstone. They immediately invited us to join them. I looked at Tilly and she smiled her agreement. They were at the brandy-and-cigar stage.

'It looks long odds on a war in the very near future, don't you think?'

'Yes,' they both nodded.

'Obviously we are going to get involved in it but there's absolutely no doubt in my mind that we shall win. We always do. And there's another thing of which I feel certain; no Germans, unless shot down from their planes or they bale out, will ever land in this country.'

Duff and Crinks looked at each other as if slightly less optimistic. Duff blew a long cloud of cigar smoke up towards the ceiling.

'Well, I hope not,' he said reflectively, 'but they *are* very strong.'

There was a sinister pause which was very quickly picked up by the intelligent Tilly. Looking at the two older men she said, 'Do you think Porchey is right when he says that the British are sure to win?'

It was Crinks who answered. He was an extraordinarily intelligent man and very truthful.

'Yes, he's probably right, because that's what happens. But, if you want my view, knowing what I do about the relative strengths of the armies and those countries who are likely to side with the Germans, I estimate that the right odds are nearer two to one on the Germans winning.'

Aware of the effect this would have on Tilly, I had visions of my bride-to-be running out before we'd reached the registrar at 9.30 a.m. Shortly after, Crinks and Duff bade us good night and we were left alone.

When we reached the end of our dinner, I took Tilly's hand.

'Of one thing I am quite sure. You are going to live in

a pretty safe part of England. Highclere has been chosen as a nursery school for that very reason.'

'I hope so,' she said.

I took Tilly back to Claridges and returned to the Ritz. In spite of the lateness of the hour, I rang my mother.

'Well, darling boy, God bless you. I hope all works out well. What are you going to do for a honeymoon?'

'Go down to Highclere – we'll arrive in time for lunch.'

'All my love and best of luck. I have a tiny gift for Tilly which I'll give her when I have the pleasure of seeing her. Are you quite sure in your heart of hearts that this is what you want?'

The question was so direct that I was lost for an answer.

'I think so,' I replied. But how could I be sure? It was a second venture for both of us.

'Well, darling boy,' Almina said, 'you know that whatever happens I shall always stand by you and I hope with all my heart that you'll both be happy.'

19
War and Peace

After a poor night's sleep I dressed, breakfasted and went round to Caxton Hall, arriving about 9.20 a.m. Shortly afterwards the registrar appeared and asked if I was Lord Carnarvon. I told him that indeed I was and he said, 'You are the first this morning. Special licence, isn't it?'

'That's right,' I replied.

'Ready in about three minutes,' said he.

Still no sign of Tilly – then suddenly she appeared on Sidney's arm, looking pale and wan. She smiled feebly and looked so miserable that I half expected her to make a sudden dash down the street.

Having completed the formalities in a few minutes, the registrar beamed, 'I wish you both the very best of luck,' and prepared for his next job fifteen minutes later.

We drove back to Claridges and there we signed the marriage settlement which seemed to cheer Tilly up quite a bit. I had a glass of champagne with my solicitor and Sidney while Tilly went to change. We motored to Highclere and had hardly stepped inside the front door when the nursery school arrived at the back. Two days later Chamberlain declared war.

When it became clear that hostilities would take place,

arrangements had been made for part of the Castle to be leased and a nursery school from London was housed here for the duration. This turned out to be a very happy arrangement for not only were some hundred evacuees – children and their attendants – kept safe and happy but there was no question of the premises being taken over by the Army or RAF, as was the case with my stud farm buildings.

The plan worked surprisingly well. The children had the whole of the top floor and the dining room and library on the ground floor. We managed very well with two small rooms next to my study as dining and sitting rooms and my staff adjusted to the invasion in wonderful style. My French chef, Monsieur Aubry, was initially burdened with feeding daily one hundred extra mouths but the co-operation within our small world was, I like to think, a tiny contribution to what was popularly known as 'the war effort'.

The children were all under five years of age and very well-behaved. They provided much amusement and I well remember when Cardy and Crinks used to come on Friday evenings to shoot on the Saturday. They had filled their pockets with sweets and would install themselves in the saloon to await the children in their pyjamas and dressing gowns trooping across to the library to bed. This became a ritual, with the children breaking line and whooping across to them, to the disgust of their prim headmistress.

Another incident which remains in my memory was the ice storm in February 1940. The children's parents liked to visit them whenever possible and generally came on Sundays. This particular Sunday they had started out in the morning, not knowing about the weather conditions that had afflicted us in the south as, of course, there were no weather forecasts for security reasons. They managed to arrive at Highclere – some forty of them – but conditions worsened with black ice forming and trees crashing down blocking all the roads and smashing the telephone lines (I lost many of the First Earl's great cedars that day): we soon had no communication with the outside world. As a result, the parents were unable to get back to London and many of them were very distressed as they had left other children at home. A few did try to climb over trees and walk to Newbury but most had to give up and stay the night.

The housekeeper mobilized mattresses and coverings and arranged dormitories for men and women. The chef and his staff worked wonders with cans of soup, biscuits and hot drinks and all were fed and warm until on Monday morning – the forestry staff having worked like beavers – we were able to get them to Newbury for trains to London.

I think the children, with their teachers, nurses and helpers alike, enjoyed Highclere. My gardens are opened for charity each year and I have been delighted when, on many of these occasions, people have come up to me and said they were here during the war, recounting their memories of happy times and have introduced their children who, if only for a few hours, enjoy what we still have to offer.

My own darling daughter Penelope spent the first part of the war in America for my friend Brose Clark and his sweet wife had begged me to let them look after her; I felt this to be a good idea, to which Catherine readily agreed. She sailed away in company with Peter Ward, Eric Dudley's younger son, both of them in the care of Penelope's beloved governess, Mlle Huc, who, I am happy to say, is very much alive to-day, retired and living in France. Unlike Penelope, Peter had nobody in America that he knew well, so Eric decided on the bright idea of sewing several large emeralds into a chamois leather bag which was placed round his waist.

Whilst over there at Foxcroft School, Penelope was invited to ride an unruly horse, quite unlike the well-mannered ponies she had ridden at home, and was run away with and thrown. This experience, unfortunately, put her off all forms of riding and she never rode again. At the age of seventeen she returned home and shortly afterwards joined the WRNS, in which she served until hostilities ceased. She looked very smart in her uniform and must have been quite the most petite in that élite company as she was only five feet tall.

Her brother, who was just over a year older, remained behind in England. He eventually joined the Royal Horse Guards, saw service in Egypt and Italy and, happily, returned safely.

But I have jumped ahead in time, away from the day I was married to Tilly. Well, October 1939 came and went; autumn set in and, with it, the phoney war. Reminding me that she must continue her convalescence from TB, Tilly suggested that now was the time for her to move to Arizona. Saddened but resigned, I kissed her goodbye and she left for New York. From newspaper reports, she seemed in no hurry to make for the desert but held court there.

Meanwhile, I had renewed my requests to the War Office for employment, this time successfully. Alan Breitmeyer got command of the 6th Cavalry Training Regiment and I became his adjutant. It was quite like old times. We were stationed at Shorncliffe.

In March I had had a bad attack of tonsilitis and was told that I must have an operation for their removal. This was duly performed in London and I very nearly died from haemorrhaging. When I came out of hospital, I was advised that a holiday in the sun would help my convalescence. I had been beseeching Tilly in letters and cables to come home, to which she finally agreed, having loved every minute of her time in Arizona with Nin Ryan. She boarded the Italian vessel *Conte di Savoia* and I met her at Genoa.

We spent a few days as a second honeymoon at the Hôtel de Paris in Monte Carlo until Tilly became bored with gambling and told me she would like to go to Paris to see her many friends, especially Noel Coward, whose flat was opposite the Ritz Hotel. Somewhat annoyed as I needed the sun and was on sick leave for that very purpose, I eventually gave way to her and we entrained for Paris and the Ritz. The food was good, there were masses of soldiers in uniform, we raced at Longchamps and went to innumerable parties. Tilly was in her seventh heaven. Easter was upon us and we attended Easter Day service in Notre Dame. I had taken the precaution of asking my servant to pack one of my uniforms and, not wishing to appear at this critical hour as a civilian, I decided to wear it. All went well until after the service when we were strolling along in the warm spring sunshine. Suddenly, from out of the crowd, an officer appeared and made his way straight towards us. He was on the Provost Marshal's staff and, saluting smartly, said, 'Excuse me interrupting you but may I see your papers and your leave warrant?'

I was nonplussed.

'I'm terribly sorry, but I'm not quite sure what you're referring to. I'm here on sick leave. I'm stationed at Shorncliffe but I've just had an operation and I've been convalescing for a few days in the south where I met my wife, Lady Carnarvon, who has just returned from America.'

The man looked at me with increasing suspicion.

'This is very irregular. You're in Paris, away from your unit, on leave, no pass?'

'Well,' I said, 'if there is any doubt in your mind, there are hundreds of people who can vouch for my story.'

'Yes, I can,' spoke up Tilly, 'he's my husband, Lord Carnarvon.'

'I realize that,' he snapped. 'I don't disbelieve you, but it is still very irregular. I shall have to report this to the War Office.'

'You're at liberty to do anything you like,' I told him.

'After all,' he continued, 'you're away from your unit, without a single identity document. You could be anybody from my point of view. You might even be a German spy.'

'Well,' I said smiling, 'any figment of the imagination is possible...'

At this, he became exceedingly angry and could hardly contain himself.

'I shall report this whole matter in detail to the War Office.'

Whether he ever did, I shall never know, as I heard not another word about it.

Two or three nights later, I had another brush with the

military, this time at a cocktail party. Colonel Lindemann (later to become Lord Cherwell and a confidant of Churchill's throughout the war) was also there and introduced me to a White Russian who was a lieutenant-colonel serving with the Deuxième Bureau.

'You know,' he said, 'you could be very useful on my staff, Lord Carnarvon. You speak excellent French which is most unusual in an Englishman.'

I thanked him politely and explained that I was Brit's adjutant at Shorncliffe and that I was also of more use in England looking after my manifold farming interests. This was the reason why I'd had to refuse an offer from the Military Secretary to go to Washington as Military Attaché to our Embassy.

With his eyes lingering on Tilly, he was not to be outdone.

'I quite understand your feelings but I must warn you I consider this matter to be so important that I may ask for your transfer.'

Tilly was furious. Indeed, it was the second time on this trip that she had been moved to anger. The first was shortly after breakfast before our visit to Notre Dame. She had made a very strict rule at the beginning of our marriage that at no time was I to enter her bedroom or dressing room without knocking first. She explained that there was nothing more unromantic than seeing a woman half dressed and covered in grease.

'I don't like it, I do not wish you to do it and I hope you understand.'

On this particular morning I forgot and, barely tapping at the door, I pushed it open. She saw me coming through the mirror of the dressing table, picked up her hairbrush and turning, hurled it straight at my head. Had I not ducked, it would have hit me between the eyes. With a crack, it smashed into the mahogany door.

'I told you never to enter my room without knocking!'

'I'm so sorry,' I murmured, beating a hasty retreat.

Jamais deux sans trois. That evening we were invited to Noel Coward's flat in the Place Vendôme. I knew him quite well but Tilly claimed him as a very close friend which indeed he was. There were several people having drinks and, in due course, Noel sat down at the piano and began playing some of his lovely tunes. We all crowded round. Various people sang and the party began to go with a swing.

I can whistle quite well and, as Noel played, I began to accompany him and everyone seemed to enjoy it until, some minutes later, I caught Tilly's furious gaze. I stopped whistling and went to find a drink. When we left the flat she turned on me.

'Leesen darling and leesen carefully. When you are in the presence of a great artist like Noel, will you kindly not indulge in your little tricks of wheestling.'

'But Noel didn't mind,' I said, 'in fact, I think he rather enjoyed it.'

'That's nothing to do with it,' she snapped.

A few days later we returned to Shorncliffe. By now, the odd bombs were beginning to fall and Tilly was working herself into a panic.

'I don't like this at all,' she complained, 'I cannot sleep and I am very worried. If I'm going to stay here, you must build me an air-raid shelter.'

I commissioned a local contractor who, for the princely sum of one hundred and eighty-five pounds, set to work in the garden of the house we had taken. I need not have bothered as Tilly had left England long before any bombs fell near the house. The only value of the air-raid shelter – which was splendidly designed – was for the storage of bombs and ammunition for the Home Guard who, happily, were destined never to use it.

Robert Taylor, my valet at the time, and Jack Gibbins, my chauffeur, had both been enrolled into the Royal Armoured Corps. Gibbins became military chauffeur to King George VI and remained with him until the end of the war. The former was subsequently badly wounded in his tank in

France. He returned to Highclere as my butler and to-day he is hale and hearty and still gives me invaluable service.

I had to refuse quite a few friends – all old cavalry officers – who wanted to join our organization. Brit was insistent, quite rightly, that anyone we took on must be of use to the 6th Cavalry Training Regiment. My dear friend, Bert Marlborough, had started his war as ADC to General Ironside. After a pleasant weekend at Blenheim, he went into his room at the War Office one Monday morning and found his chief had been sacked and he also was out of a job. He asked me if I could take him on. Brit agreed somewhat reluctantly and insisted that he must work hard if he wished to remain with us. After he had been there twenty-four hours, he was sent out on a scheme with his squadron and returned so stiff and sore that he could hardly hobble into the Mess.

After lunch, he drove down to the sea-front and strolled towards a bench to rest in the sunshine. He was suddenly aroused from his reveries by a corporal and two soldiers pointing their rifles at him and telling him to put his hands up and come to the guard room with them. When he got there, protesting vigorously that he was the Duke of Marlborough, attached to the 6th Cavalry Training Regiment, and not a German spy, he was held until I went down and bailed him out.

A couple of days later I was told that Winston was coming down to see us, accompanied by quite a few high-ranking officers. Brit and I took them round the lines and Winston, leaning on his stick, made the following remarks.

'Of all the ridiculous locations to be training a cavalry unit, I cannot imagine any place less suitable. You are near to Lympne aerodrome and if one bomb were to fall among your horses, they would stampede and gallop over the cliffs like the Gadarene swine. I shall have you moved immediately.'

As good as his word, three days later we were *en route* for Sherwood Forest. Here we established a camp under canvas and proceeded to train vigorously.

After a few weeks, the GOC Northern Command decided to look us over. He was an elderly gentleman, steeped in the traditions of the past. We laid on a guard with drawn swords to receive him. He drove to the Mess tent and, after a glass of port, inspected the lines.

'What lovely horses you have,' he said. 'Those over there are chestnuts? Is that correct?'

'Yes, General, that's correct.'

'Is it not the case that Lord Lonsdale, when he was hunting, always rode chestnuts?'

'He did, General.'

'Now, what about those, are they black?'

'No, General, we call them brown.'

'They look very black to me.'

I tried to explain the difference.

'Oh, I see,' he nodded gravely. 'I've been giving a great deal of thought to your role and I envisage the following.'

'Yes, General,' we prompted him.

'Well, what I think is this. If you were to send out patrols fairly regularly, when we get a warning of parachutists dropping – which is very likely – I think your men could play a very useful part in despatching them. I envisage that with the points of their swords they will be able to transfix them as they are coming in to land.'

On the point of hysterics, I turned to Alan Breitmeyer. His face was a study. He was simply aghast and almost unbelieving. Suddenly, he found his tongue.

'Well, General, it's a very interesting idea, but I think we might do a bit better if you were to arm us with lances as opposed to swords. Then we'll be able to reach up higher to get at 'em.'

The news on all fronts was bad; the miracle of Dunkirk was achieved. But as each week went by, with the Press reports daily suggesting impending invasion, my dear Tilly became more and more frightened. She decided to take a trip to Ireland to stay with her friend Adele Cavendish. Frankly, I was relieved. Her fear was understandable for she had no love of the Germans and having only recently surrendered her security in America to come back to front-line Britain, she was now terrified.

Six weeks later she returned to London and I asked Brit for a forty-eight hour pass in order to meet her. We had taken a room at the Ritz and I joined her there. It was at breakfast, looking radiant and well, that she produced the cable. It was not for some time that I learnt of its origin. Phone calls from England to America by civilians were forbidden, but in neutral Ireland communication with the States was still possible and certain transatlantic calls had been exchanged.

'Darling Porchey, I must show you,' she bubbled, 'I've had the most wonderful offer. Do read it . . . isn't it marvellous?'

By this time, I was becoming inured to shocks, so much so that I took the cable in a resigned and somewhat sceptical mood. It was an offer for a run-of-play contract which would be produced on Broadway and in which Tilly was offered a starring role. Details of the salary were given, together with the suggestion that should the play turn out to be a great success, a contract with a major film studio would follow. Then came the crunch: 'YOUR IMMEDIATE DECISION VITAL STOP REHEARSALS COMMENCING FOUR WEEKS' TIME.'

'But Tilly, you've only just come back to England. If you return to America now you may be there for the duration. The war may go on for ages.'

Tilly pouted. 'You must let me go, darling. I'm terrified to stay here. I am an Austrian and I have Jewish blood. I think the Germans will land here soon and then do you know what will happen? Hermann Goering will rape me and probably kill me.'

She spread her hands in a dramatic gesture as if imploring me to save her life. Unfortunately, I replied without thinking.

'What a glorious death!'

'You fool, I might have expected something like that from you. I am trying to tell you my life is in danger and that

I have a wonderful chance for a success on the stage and all you do is to make fun of me.'

'Think,' I said, 'if you go back to America now, everyone will consider that you are yellow, that you have cut and run. What will our friends say? What will people think of you?'

'Look, Porchey,' she said earnestly, 'I believe the Germans will win this war. If I go to America I can earn some money. Then, when the war is over, you can escape from England and join me in the States where I'll have a home ready for you. You can't beat the Germans. Look what they have done to France.'

It was now my turn to be angry. I had had enough.

'Look here, Tilly, it's been interesting hearing your views but I don't agree with them.'

She sat looking at me as if I were mad.

'Well, *I* want to leave.'

'Very well,' I said quietly, 'I must think it over for two or three days and then I shall let you know my decision.'

Of course, I had made an error. We had only been married nine months and had spent little time together. It was Almina, now a grand old lady, who characteristically summed up the situation. Her words were short and to the point, their truth undeniable: 'Let the silly bitch go! She will only prove to be a hindrance to the war effort if she stays here.' This, in fact, was not as easy to arrange as one might expect for already there was a general exodus to Canada of mothers and their children.

It was a very hot day when Tilly and I set out to obtain the exit visa for her to leave the country. I had taken her passport and stood in the queue as I felt sure that in her delicate state of health she would probably have fainted in the gruelling heat. As expected, the official issuing the exit permits said that according to her passport she had just returned from a six-month stay in the United States and that he could not let her go again when there were so many deserving cases and very limited accommodation on the *Empress of Britain*. At this stage I told him that I considered she would be of no help to the war effort and strongly advised him to give her the exit visa. He stamped her passport without further comment. Tilly was overjoyed and she returned to the Ritz in high spirits.

By now the inevitable decision had been taken that horses had no place in the world of blitzkrieg and low-flying aircraft. All cavalry units had been mechanized. The Battle of Britain having been won and the fear of imminent invasion lifted, Britain became a vast training camp with tanks tearing up the countryside, assault troops scaling the rocky headlands and waves of infantry making attacks on isolated farms, villages and townships. Inevitably, damage to civilian property would occur and I was appointed to be the Assistant Director, Claims, for Southern Command, whose two primary tasks were, firstly, to obviate unnecessary damage by troops and military personnel and, secondly, to make adequate compensation when such damage occurred.

When Alex returned triumphantly from North Africa to become GOC Southern Command, he sent for me and explained that he attached great importance to the task I had been given. 'With this tremendous influx of Canadian, American and Commonwealth troops,' he said, 'it is vital that we retain the goodwill of the people. After all, the farmers are growing the food which we desperately need and unthinking damage can easily destroy their morale. Every ton of food grown is a ton less that has to come in by convoy. Now Porchey, if you have any difficulty with senior officers under my command don't hesitate to come and see me here.'

I never took advantage of the offer. Not only was it in the main unnecessary, but I much preferred to paddle my own canoe. One of the few rows that took place was with an American colonel and arose over the preservation of the Beckhampton gallops. Together with my American liaison officer, I had gently explained that we had marked off the gallops so that his men could easily avoid them.

'Look here, Colonel,' he snapped, 'what the hell are we

over here for? We've come across the Atlantic to beat those God-damned Germans and if it means my tanks having to go across your God-damned gallops – well – they'll just go across 'em! I'm not aiming to hold back my men for a bunch of racehorse owners. So now you've got it straight, Colonel whatever-your-name-is.'

My American liaison officer tried to intervene but was shut up smartly by his superior officer.

'Very well,' I said, 'but before I leave this office, there are a couple of points that I think you should know. First, we have had to fight the Germans for two years now without your assistance and, grateful as we are to receive it, please don't think you're conducting a one-man crusade. Secondly, those gallops have probably been in existence a good deal longer than your country. They are part of our heritage and we need to protect them. There are thousands of acres on either side of them on which your tanks are free to train. Surely your troops can be made to avoid these gallops. Good-day to you, Colonel.'

As we walked out, my liaison officer found his tongue.

'I'm dreadfully sorry about this, Colonel, but I can tell you one thing. Senior to me he may be, but I guarantee he'll be back in Omaha within thirty-six hours from now. I'm going straight to his base commander and I can only apologize for his damned bad manners.'

He was as good as his word. The following day the man was sent home at 5 a.m.

Our activities increased to a crescendo as the Allied invasion armies assembled in the south of England. Damage throughout the area was inevitable and it was our job to investigate and satisfy the myriad claims.

In July 1945, like many another British soldier, my turn came to put away my uniform for the last time. Before doing so, I attended a last conference at Milford Manor near Salisbury. It took place on Wednesday 4 July at 11 a.m. I have retained an extract from the minutes of the meeting which was something of an embarrassment to endure, but the compliments paid me warmed my heart and made me feel that even I, whose life in the main had been devoted to the pleasures of a peacetime existence, could at least render some small service.

The Director of Claims from the War Office said,

> I am sure that no-one will wish this last conference under Lord Carnarvon's command to pass without telling him how much has been appreciated the firm and benevolent way in which he has guided everyone through the last sixteen or seventeen months.
>
> Lord Carnarvon's friendship with General Morgan and the American Chief of Staff has been of the greatest value to us all, particularly during the days when pressure of work was at its highest pitch around D-Day. Certainly, speaking for the staff at Milford Manor, I can say that Lord Carnarvon is regarded with very real affection as a unique AD Claims and I propose that this meeting record its deep appreciation of him during his tenure of office.

Apart from the ending of the war, the happiest event for me in 1945 was the marriage, on 21 April, of my darling daughter to Gerrit van der Woude, at Highclere. He was an American citizen who had obtained a dispensation from the President allowing him and several other US citizens to serve with the British Army without swearing the oath of allegiance to the King. Their marriage has proved to be a truly happy one, blessed by three charming children.

20
Love and Laughter

Now that the war was over I renewed my efforts to persuade Tilly to return to me but she seemed most reluctant to do so. I had spent over six hundred pounds in Western Union cables since she had left in July 1940 but to no avail. I arranged with her solicitors to divorce her for desertion and stated that I would pay her two thousand pounds a year after the divorce had been made absolute and she agreed not to contest the case.

Whilst I was in the witness box the judge asked, 'For what reason did you commit adultery when you had never stopped trying to get your wife to return to you?'

I replied, 'Your Lordship is famed for your wisdom throughout the whole of the legal world and to this particular question I can only reply the lusts of the flesh.'

This answer was received with much applause from the public gallery.

'I have never received a better reply from a witness than the one you have just given me,' said the judge. 'Nevertheless, it has become quite obvious to me that I can no longer continue to hear your case, so I shall arrange for another judge to hear your petition at a later date.'

My answer had cost me very dear. In evidence, I had put

in a discretionary statement to the learned judge naming a well-known and very charming lady who, in her turn, told me that she had been compromised by me and asked me for fifty thousand pounds. I told her that I was not going to be blackmailed and gave her a golden handshake of ten thousand. Tilly's lawyers jumped for joy as they said the tables had now been very neatly turned on me: Tilly could divorce me now and would surely get a great deal more than the two thousand a year which she had accepted so readily shortly before the case had been heard.

Six months later I went before another judge. I well remember darling Tilly, dressed in black with no make-up on, standing in the witness box.

'Lady Carnarvon, I have carefully read and made myself thoroughly acquainted with all that has transpired in the divorce proceedings between you and your husband. It was indeed a lucky break for you when the first hearing was adjourned and you, who had willingly agreed not to contest the case, have since had the ammunition to reverse the proceedings and are now suing your husband, who has not contested the case. As for your claim for maintenance, I am not going to increase this from what you originally accepted, namely two thousand pounds per year, and I shall make an order that if you remarry you will only get fifteen hundred.'

I was so amused by the short shrift which Tilly had received, and which she so richly deserved, that when I left the court with Philip Freer we went to the Savoy Grill and split a bottle of Bollinger to celebrate the end of a thoroughly unpleasant case.

Winston went to the country and I threw myself into the hurly-burly of politics, determined to do everything possible to bring about a Conservative victory. But it was while I was addressing a public meeting at Devizes that I sensed the first faint whiff of defeat in the air. Whereas the Conservative Central Office seemed blissfully confident, I could not but notice the underlying hostility of the audience which was something I had never before encountered. My next meeting took place in Portsmouth and, at that particular gathering of some four thousand people, I could hardly make myself heard as there was a heckler wearing a swastika armband shouting that I was a friend of 'that damned tyrant, Winston Churchill'. I telephoned the Central Office that evening warning them that I feared we were certain to lose the election. Immediately after the results were known, I received a telegram from Winston thanking me for my help, concluding by saying 'how right you were, dear Porchey'.

I was saddened and depressed at the country's rejection of the man who had steered them to victory. It was only with hindsight that I understood their motivation and could recognize the underlying currents of socialism that were sweeping in with the returning members of the forces. They had fought the war and won it; they were entitled to their opinions and had registered them in no uncertain fashion.

For my part, I decided to go to South America with a view to selling British bloodstock and acquiring some much needed currency to help the Exchequer.

On my return to England I set about sorting out the many problems left by the war. The paddocks in my stud farm had been ploughed from 1939 onwards to grow a succession of food crops by order of the Government and the woodlands had been ravaged to provide pit props and larch for the construction of landing craft; nearly a million cubic feet of timber had been taken. It was a lengthy process getting the stud back to good pastures and in 1947 I started to replant the woodlands under a dedication scheme which will ensure a supply of mature timber not only for the needs of the estate but for the nation to use whenever it may be required.

Throughout the war I was very fortunate to be able to leave my affairs in the capable hands of Miss Stubbings who had come to Highclere in 1937 as my Private Secretary. When war appeared to be imminent, she began to understudy Marcus Wickham-Boynton with a view to taking over the affairs of the estate and stud farm when he joined the

Welsh Guards in 1940. Her wide interest in everything to do with the land, farming and forestry, to say nothing of her knowledge of many aspects of the law and economics made her invaluable. She could hold her own in any business discussions whether with ministry officials, valuers, accountants or lawyers and was held in the greatest respect and affection by my staff and tenants, as well as my family and friends. In addition to formally qualifying as a Land Agent, she proved herself to be more than capable in dealing with my stud farm and bloodstock business. She is still with me and long may this happy state continue.

As the war receded into the distance I was gradually able to resume my normal life, shooting, racing and paying my yearly visits to America and other parts of the world. It was during one of these visits that I went to stay in Dallas, Texas, with my friend Gete Green and her husband W.A.Green (known as WAG), who owned the second largest department store in the town, Nieman Marcus being the largest. Whilst staying with them, I was invited to have dinner in the Petroleum Club, which was the equivalent of Boodles in London. Every week about twenty members dined at 7.30 p.m. and the menu, as far as I could gather, never varied: it was always a huge steak and a mound of potatoes, washed down with copious draughts of claret and champagne, followed by cheese and biscuits. Immediately coffee had been served, they usually sat down to mammoth games of gin rummy, played for colossal stakes, and I well remember my host telling me that as a rule they settled up once a year and that the results could well be that Mr A had won a million dollars from Mr B and Mr C which, of course, meant nothing to these immensely rich tycoons, one of whom, I know, had started life earning five dollars an hour wielding a jack-hammer in the oil fields.

The following day, the Greens asked me if I would go with them to Fort Worth where a big function was taking place to thank Mr Hunt, father of the present Bunker Hunt, for his generosity in giving some eighty million dollars to build a wing of a hospital in Fort Worth. Old man Hunt had originally owned a small farm of one hundred and twenty-three acres on which he had grazed about twenty cows; in those days he had not even been able to sign his name. Then people prospecting for oil had found a great stream of the precious stuff underneath his farm which had made him enormously rich.

It was a lovely hot day and many fulsome speeches were made by those present saying what a wonderful citizen and marvellous man Mr Hunt was and the vast crowd of people who were sitting on the grass were bored to tears. At the very end, I was asked to say a few words, so I leapt to my feet and said, 'Ladies and gentlemen, I have never seen so many intoxicating women or so many intoxicated men.' This really brought them to their feet. I then went on to say that Mr Hunt had been a very lucky man to have become so rich fortuitously and it was nice that he should be so generous. This pleased Mr Hunt immensely.

When we were alone together later, he asked me if I knew a really good doctor in New York who could get rid of a tape-worm from which he suffered. I suggested my friend, Ben Kean, who practised in New York, and told Hunt that I was quite sure Ben would be able to remove his lodger if he put himself in his hands. Subsequently, he went to see Ben and said, 'The moment you can show me the head of this tape-worm, I shall give you one hundred thousand dollars *plus* an oil well.' Ben readily agreed but said that Mr Hunt must do exactly as he told him. Within three days Ben had fulfilled his contract, and I believe his oil well is still bringing him in a tidy revenue.

Back once more in England I continued with my breeding and racing, but the event which gave me the greatest pleasure during the fifties was, of course, the marriage of my son, Henry, who was also known as Porchester in his turn. In July 1955 he was driving me down to Newmarket in his car when he surprised me by saying, 'Papa, I am going to America to stay with Oliver Wallop in Wyoming for about a month.'

'What on earth are you going to do there?' I asked him.

'Papa,' he said, 'do you remember Jeannie Wallop?'

'No,' I replied.

'Oh, Papa, you *must* remember her. She sat next to you at lunch at Highclere this summer.'

As he had brought so many charming young ladies to my house, I had not at the time realized that this was The One.

He then said, 'You have often told me there is nothing like having a look at them in their own surroundings.'

I heartily agreed and so we arranged that if he had popped the question and had been accepted, he would send me a cable saying, 'ALL OKAY'. On receipt of this, I told him, I would arrange a dinner party at the Ritz Hotel to celebrate his engagement. When it finally arrived, I invited thirty-six people to dinner. My mother presided at one table of twelve, my daughter at another and I at the third. After dinner, I told the assembled company the great news that my son had become engaged and was shortly to marry Jeannie Wallop. It really was a revelation to see the expression on the faces of some of the assembled company who, I feel sure, had long hoped they would be the lady of his choice.

One or two who had blanched at the news quickly recovered their *sang-froid* and we all drank to the long life and happiness of the couple which, I am glad to say, has indeed come to pass. I attended their wedding in New York in January 1956 and met, for the first time, several of my daughter-in-law's relations, one of whom was Bishop Moore. If my memory serves me right, he officiated at their wedding.

Blessed by three glorious children, this has proved to be one of the truly happy marriages which, alas, are so rare in this day and age.

At one time, my son Henry was asked by Princess Margaret to help her get together a cast to perform a play called *The Frog* by Edgar Wallace. Princess Margaret was the co-director and Henry played the part of Inspector Elk. This was the star role which had been portrayed so memorably by dear old Gordon Harker. Gordon was kind enough to have Henry down to stay a night with him at his flat in Brighton when he gave him invaluable help on how to play it.

Others in the cast of twenty-five were Billy Wallace, Patrick Plunket, Raine Legge, Maureen Dufferin, Douglas Fairbanks, Andrew Devonshire, Kate Smith, Judy Montagu, Colin Tennant, Mary-Lou Hennessy, Dominic Elliot and Billy Ednam. I played the part of a nightclub proprietor called Spike and during the run of the play I kept open house in my dressing room at the Scala Theatre which I shared with my son. All the cast kept popping in at odd times for champagne and caviare sandwiches and a good time was had by all.

At the dress rehearsal, which was performed on the Monday of Epsom week, four hundred seats were reserved in the stalls for friends of the cast and the general public were allowed to come in free. At the end of the first act, members of the cast took round collecting boxes for charity and collected just under £800 in cash which was an excellent beginning to a most successful week.

I was lucky enough to be able to bring out the fact that Never Say Die had won the Derby on the Wednesday night when the Royal Family were there. When proposing a toast to all Frogs, I said, 'Here's luck to all Frogs, Never Say Die.' I saw Princess Margaret lean across to the Queen and say 'Porchey is gagging'. Her sister nodded and applauded vigorously.

Except for the fact that the public were greatly amused when Billy Wallace had to make love to Raine Legge, all the rest of the performance was as perfect as any amateur production could hope to be. Please remember that from start to finish we had to rehearse at odd times in friends' houses in London and only once did we have the opportunity of doing so on a cold stage at the Savoy Theatre shortly before we were due to open. At the end of the week, the Invalid Children's Aid Association benefited by around £11,000 which was no mean achievement.

After all this excitement I went off to Nassau to stay with my daughter, Penelope. Whilst I was there, a cable arrived from my trainer, Atty Corbett, suggesting that I might like to buy a yearling colt, an own brother to Scotch Fusilier by March Past out of Jojo, for one thousand pounds. Realizing that the price was modest, I cabled back that I would buy the yearling, informed my office accordingly and asked them to send a cheque to the owner.

When I returned to Highclere, I immediately went down to the stud to see Devonish, my very experienced stud groom, in order that we could look at the colt together.

'Good morning, m'lord.'

'What's the new yearling like?'

'Hm, pretty miserable in comparison with our own yearlings.'

'Really, what's wrong?'

'Well, he's a skinny little thing, very unimpressive. I don't know what you'll think, but that's my opinion anyway.'

'Oh well, no doubt he'll change.'

'I don't think he's had over much to eat just recently; he came in a cattle float.'

What this had to do with it, I could not imagine. However we walked over to the paddock and had a look at him. Certainly he was skinny, but very well made and seemed to have an equable temperament. He was a hard bay and looked an early sort. By the autumn, he had improved out of all recognition. We broke him in carefully, as we always do with our yearlings. Then we sent him to Corbett. In due course I went to Compton and asked my trainer what he thought of him.

'Oh,' he said, 'I like this horse now I've got him, but he's a proper little monkey. He'll kick anybody off, but he's full of guts.'

At Christmas, I again went to see this yearling whom I had named Queen's Hussar and watched him doing a canter. I was well satisfied with his progress. After Christmas I went abroad and when I returned went down immediately to see Atty.

'How's Queen's Hussar going?'

'Fine,' he said, 'I'm thinking of giving him an outing at Windsor.'

'At Windsor? Surely that's only in a week's time?'

'Well, he needs a race badly.'

There were only five runners and Lester Piggott rode him. He was always odds on and won very easily. Lester's comment: 'I don't know what he's beaten today, possibly nothing. He's pretty green at present but nevertheless I'm sure he can go. There's no doubt of that.'

The next time he ran was at Epsom where he won and I had a good bet on him. He then went on to win the Washington Singer Stakes at Newbury. The following year he won the Lockinge Stakes and the Sussex Stakes and as a four-year-old he ended up winning the Cavendish Stakes at Sandown and then he went to stud. With his breeding and his performance on the racetrack, I thought Queen's Hussar would do rather well as a stallion, but not a bit of it. In the first year, we had the greatest difficulty in finding sufficient mares at around four hundred pounds a service; we needed approximately twenty-five of them. The following year it was even worse. The third year we decided to reduce the stud fee to two hundred and fifty pounds and a lot of scrubbing brushes arrived.

Then an odd winner or two began to appear but nothing outstanding until, mercifully for me, a mare arrived owned by John Hislop, named La Paiva. The result of that match, as all the world knows, was a horse that won seventeen races, two hundred and forty-three thousand, nine hundred and twenty-six pounds, and whose name is written indelibly in the history of great racehorses: Queen's Hussar had begat the famous Brigadier Gerard. However, the final chapter of his story has yet to be told for even as I recount this in my seventy-eighth year, his career is not ended and it is yet possible that some other good horses may be produced. Time alone will tell.

* * *

I have loved every moment of my life and taken great joy in my family and friends. Perhaps I have not always loved wisely, but certainly quite well. I have witnessed the passing of an era that spans man's first powered flight to the moment when he stepped on the moon. Who could ask for more?

I have met some of the greatest men of this century and been privileged to call them my friends. I am now left with two abiding impressions. The first is the ever-recurring sorrow occasioned by the passing of my friends but to counteract this there is the joy I find in the love and affection of my grandchildren. They skip gaily into a new life, a changing world, the staggering implications of which defy my mental capacity. Yet, when I walk out on to the lawn at Highclere and behond my cedars, I realize that all things are relative and nature will endure despite all the changes man may endeavour to bring about.

If, by my writings, I have brought alive a little of the past, caused a ripple or two of laughter and illumined for my grandchildren some portion of my life and adventures, then perhaps the exercise has not been misplaced. I have tried to be honest but not unkind.

When I see the delightful young people of to-day, I am full of hope for the future. Farewell, my friends.